LIFT UP YOUR HEARTS

LIFT UP YOUR HEARTS:

Story Telling, Heart of Community

To Jean, thank you

M. Laurel Buck

M. Laurel Buck

Shoreline

Cover design: Sarah Robinson
Editing: Shanti Maharaj and Drew McKevitt
Published in Canada by Shoreline, 23 Ste-Anne
Ste-Anne-de-Bellevue, Quebec H9X 1L1
514-457-5733
shoreline@sympatico.ca   www.shorelinepress.ca

Dépôt légal: Library and Archives Canada
and Bibliothèque nationale de Quebec

Library and Archives Canada Cataloguing in Publication
Buck, M. Laurel, 1927-
Lift up your hearts : story telling, heart of community / M. Laurel Buck.
ISBN 1-896754-52-X
1. Buck, M. Laurel, 1927-. 2. Calgary (Alta.)-Biography.
3. Ireland-Description and travel. 4. Storytelling.
I. Title.

FC3697.26.B82A3 2006   971.23'3803092   C2006-905938-1

DEDICATION

I dedicate this book to my John, the listener,
always the first one to know which way the wind is blowing
for the writer at work.

I also dedicate this to our seven grandchildren,
two generations among them, but still first cousins.
At ages 30, 28, 17, 15, 11, 7 and 5,
they enrich our lives
with their wonderful and varied perspectives on life.

We are equally enriched through our sons and daughters-in-law
and our one grand-daughter-in-law ~ our grandson's wife.
I write for them all.

Laurel Canning Buck

CONTENTS

FOREWORD

"Only connect." In E.M. Forster's view, connecting with others is the prime directive when it comes to finding our place in the world. To that maxim, *Lift Up Your Hearts* adds: only have an open heart, and you will connect.

A break in those connections will surely leave you broken-hearted, too. Losing a home, leaving people behind, having them leave you, is something Laurel knows and wrote about in *Stream of Memory*.

In the end, though, she finds that chances to connect are all around, even if you're a stranger in a strange land. Years of traveling have given rise to vignettes of brief intimacy among fellow wayfarers on the road. Differences in culture, language, or age all fall away in a heart-to-heart meeting.

Even the gap between tourist and local, student and teacher, newcomer and deep-rooted resident disappears in the face of gracious interest in the personhood of the other. So, too, can heartfelt connection surpass the passage of time, through the rediscovery of old letters from loved ones or a note from an acquaintance whose life touched ours. New-found cousins serve as a reminder of the ways in which our lives are involved one with another.

Only open your heart and you will connect to the holiness of everyday lived experience. Those moments of connection that punctuate the story of our lives are treasures too valuable to be kept to ourselves. Instead Laurel turns them into insights to be shared and used to uplift the hearts of others ~ yet another way of fostering connection, this time between storyteller and reader.

Sarah Buck

PROLOGUE

Each title chosen by a writer of memoirs reveals a little of her life, the book itself being a chronicle of a biographical nature.

My first book was *Stream of Memory: Reflections of Megantic County*. The stream that ran through the cellar of the first home I remember, my maternal grandparents' farm home, became an image of memories surfacing. Indeed, as I wrote, that stream became a floodgate of memories mixed with happy days, the sadness of loss and ultimately, the joy of healing.

My second book was *Roots beneath the Pavement:: A Tribute to Verdun by one of her Reluctant Children, 1930s-1940s*. My parents and many of their generation experienced an exodus from their Megantic farm community during the Great Depression. At the age of five, I began the traumatic transition from farm child to city child. It was not until my grandmotherly age that I could contemplate writing about Verdun and ultimately uncover my roots there.

My third book was *The Spiral Road: Reflections of Life Journey and Travel, turned Pilgrimage*. It was in the writing of this book that I began to reflect upon the breadth of my life journey, including the travels John and I had made to Ireland. I came to the conclusion that rather than the closed circle being a symbol of life journey, the Celtic idea of the spiral ~ a complex, continuous circularity ~ more fully expresses the essence of the journey. Indeed, life journey is a pilgrimage that can be found also in travel as we seek to communicate with people whose place we have entered.

My fourth book, *Lift Up your Hearts: Story Telling, Heart of Community* is the most recent in a series of life stories. It begins with a question: What would it take to build community expressed through neighbourliness in such a hectic society as we experience today? Stressful work places, gridlocked roads, long commutes morning and evening, and anxiety about the state of the world leave little time to live a life. What has always been at the heart of community, the cultivation of neighbourliness, is the human need to communicate with one another. That is what story telling means, a human activity that leads to a sense of belonging.

In retrospect, I see that the very title that I chose, *Lift Up Your Hearts*, gave me encouragement to recollect life stories. For example, I began to explore boxes full of letters untouched for years. All are precious, especially one from my father written to his grandsons in February 1977 ~ a month, as it turned out, before his death. His letter was full of love of family, of whimsical touches of humour and of looking forward to spring.

Recently, a friend said to me, "Laurel, your life is an open book. I have to say that many of your experiences are like my own." I found her words encouraging, for they express the very essence of the heart of community, the sharing of biography.

Laurel Canning Buck

THEN AND NOW

From Story Telling to Story Writing

Behind my written stories lies a well-spring of oral tradition that flowed naturally from the elders in my old Irish-Quebec community to the listening child I was. In their telling, they brought to light not only days gone by, but the 'one day at a time' happenings that spin the tales of our lives. Face to face with one another, we were caught up in that particular emotional intimacy born of words on the tongue and sounds of the voice, drawing us into the heart of community.

I have been a story teller ever since. When I was still a child, I told stories to my young sister, to my playmates while 'playing house' and as a young woman, to our children. After teaching for several years, I was at home for fourteen helping to raise our four sons; the first three were born in three years and a bit, the fourth, four years later.

After our last child entered grade one, I spent nearly twenty years, twice a week, teaching adults the matriculation level of English in the Calgary Public School Board's Adult Education (Academic area). While my students were the principal learners, my experience of teaching the curriculum after so many years was like meeting old friends again: the novel; the essay; drama, including Shakespeare; poetry; how to write a well-structured essay; as well as how to tell a story.

With often three generations in my classroom during the 1970s and 1980s, I encouraged my students to draw upon their reasons for returning to school and some of their experiences that had brought them to make this decision; in other words, to tell their own stories. In turn they would ask me questions about my own return to the classroom after so many years. Soon story telling and story listening developed and, what any serious teacher hopes for, a community of learners began.

Occasionally during those years, students would say, "Why don't you write stories?" And I would reply, "Because I teach and I don't have time to write." On the last day of one of my classes, one

13

student came forward and handed me the gift of a book. "This is for you. I think you should read it." The title was *Maybe You Should Write a Book.* In hindsight this was an omen of what was to come.

In 1984, however, a year before I retired from teaching, while still in my fifties, I enrolled in a course at the University of Calgary in Canadian Fiction, thus becoming a part-time student and a teacher, still in Adult Education. My students got a great charge out of my apparent crossing the line between them and me, asking me probing questions about how I liked writing essays and what kind of marks I was getting. In other words, they began to sound like me in the role of teacher!

I decided to retire early because I wanted to pursue more courses at the U of C. During World War II, at seventeen, I had entered McGill University. I graduated in 1948 and begun to teach, my first position an educator in my old Quebec community. To recollect the young girl I had been all those years ago, in the light of the age I now was, made me feel almost motherly toward that memory of myself. On that last day before my retirement, my students and I lingered, not wanting to part just yet. There they stood, three generations of them, having learned as much from one another as from the prescribed curriculum, an experience that I shared with them.

When the last one had gone, I began to gather up my books and clear my desk. When I was done, I placed my hands on the desk and looked down at its cleared surface. I was surprised to see that both my hands had turned blue! I began to massage them and soon they resumed their regular appearance, the blue not recurring again.

The following year, 1986, a few months before I was to begin my Master's Studies at the university, I had an angina attack, apparently as a result of a coronary artery that was ninety percent blocked because of a previously unknown inherited condition. The procedure to reverse the blockage, angioplasty, was completely successful. Great advances over the years in new approaches to treatment based on ongoing research continue to help many like me.

I completed my studies, having had to learn part-way into my first year how to type ~ a new regulation at the university (no more handwritten essays!). My son, Martin, my mentor, recommended that I learn to type on a word processor rather than a typewriter and to prove the point, provided me with a typing program called *Letter Fall*. I finally mastered the challenge of moving from handwritten essays to placing both hands on a keyboard and composing while looking at a screen.

The business of writing essays for professors had occupied me for about three years. Once I had graduated, the tools were already in place, and now I had the time to think about writing my own stories. Not only that, I began to find my motivation, for I had experienced a brush with my own mortality, causing me to reflect, among other things, on the gift of story telling my people had bestowed on me.

Moreover, I had the book my student had placed in my hands. For its very title suggested a way forward where the written word on the page might come to life in the light of the story telling I had always known. If by chance the stories might turn into a book, then, I hoped, there would arise another kind of community between the writer and the readers. At last I was ready to begin and, indeed, in time the stories began to well up just as in oral story telling, for they came from the same place!

And Now to Begin Again...

Forty years ago, in 1965, my husband, John, and I and our four young sons moved from Montreal to Calgary, John having accepted a position as associate priest at Christ Church in Elbow Park. At that time Calgary was a small city of about 275,000. We lived at first in a rented house facing Christ Church Park, but some time later moved into a house on 8th Street, close to 38th Avenue where we have lived ever since. From the beginning, this western part of Elbow Park felt like a village with a hill at its back, a river nearby, Elbow Park School with a steeple on top and beautiful Christ Church at the heart. Its wonderful bells have been ringing throughout our part of the valley for over ninety years, speaking to the surrounding neigbourhood, the newcomers as well as longtime residents, of the Good News, ever old, ever new.

We soon found that our welcome was twofold. Drawn into the life of Christ Church, we experienced the spiritual depth of the community at worship, broadened in three Bible study groups that lasted for many years. But we also discovered that the parishioners enjoyed good parties that meant eating together, enjoying music and dancing. And there were always at least two to three generations. That is still the case today!

But as in a village, the wider community, while it included many Christ Church people, was made up of equally welcoming neighbours, taking time to cross the street or the back lane and stand to talk with us. John and I were not yet out of our thirties, our sons ranging in age from twelve to five. Many of our neighbours were of the same age as we; some, as we, had originated in the eastern part of our country. It was that western hospitality that drew them and us in and made us at home. Soon we had joined with our Alberta-born contemporaries.

Consequently, John and I have grown old along with our neighbours ~ who became our close friends, while our sons grew to manhood, married wives who were raised in the west and together have given us seven grandchildren, all born in Calgary. Indeed, three of our sons and families live close by, prompting one neighbour to say, "It's getting to be like Buck Village." In fact, ours is not the only family to experience the return of their offspring to Elbow Park where they were raised.

In 2005, Calgary's population is close to one million. Given the frenetic pace of life, demanding workplaces and the troubled times we live in, the deeply rewarding experience of community is missing from the lives of many. I find myself reflecting, What would it take in such a society to begin building a culture of neighbourliness, signifying community? As poet Robert Frost wrote, "When a friend calls to me from the road... I don't stand still... and shout 'What is it?' No... I go up to the stone wall for a friendly visit." Human experience says Begin Here.

The Challenge of Change

Many changes in our Elbow Valley have occurred in the last few years. Some of our neighbours who once were the oldest generation are no longer with us and those of us who were young forty years ago are now the oldest, some of us still in our same homes. These changes are in the natural order of things. But some of our contemporaries, living in houses that once accommodated two or more generations, have sold their properties and moved into alternative housing.

Then began a practice that has become a phenomenon of our age, not only in this country, but elsewhere in the western world: developers demolished the homes to clear the valuable large lots for new three-storey houses. The effect upon the remaining longtime residents, not all of them in old age, was traumatic. Indeed, a grieving time followed, felt by two generations. For the loss of our elders meant the disappearance of a vital segment of our community's history that represented the close relationship of three generations as in a village. And it was compounded by the disappearance of their houses and gardens, which often occurred in quick succession, leaving gaping holes in the ground.

17

However, in time, our tradition of neighbourliness has begun to stir. It has been helped in large part by already neighbourly relations between the present elders and some younger people who, in the vanguard from elsewhere, were happy to settle in a community that is urban, yet like a village. For example, one young woman and her husband, experienced in intergenerational relationships from childhood, have for several years welcomed a good cross-section of us to an annual Christmas party. It was time, at last, for us elder ones to approach the new crop of recent arrivals. Like Frost's character we "went up to the stone wall (in more ways than one) for a friendly visit."

A response has begun to grow: a young woman wheels her wheelbarrow down the lane last spring to admire our old garden. In it she already has a collection of perennials. "I'm asking the neighbours if I may have some sprigs from their established gardens to plant in my newly dug flower bed," she says. I open the gate.

Another young woman with two little girls opens her gate to go inside. It just happens that I'm working in my garden. I call to her to say hello and introduce myself. I learn her name and the children's, who have beautiful names (Shea and Clare) and I tell them so. The mother smiles at me and passes through the gate, the little girls lingering for a moment. They follow her, then turn to wave at me.

One day, by our back fence, I come face to face with their very busy father. He is walking with a new puppy called "Paddy." Paddy crosses the lane to say hello. In a matter of seconds, my neighbour is telling me about his Irish ancestors who came to Ontario long ago. Recently, some of the newcomers on our street have begun to comment, "You have been here longer than any of us," sometimes followed by questions about days gone by. For them, it appears we put a face on history and that could mean that sharing one another's stories is not far behind.

Lately, there have been further signs of response. The young woman of the wheelbarrow sent out invitations to tea to surrounding neighbours. A couple of seniors, younger than John and I, held two dinner parties last winter. The guests represented the new and the old, giving rise to mutual story telling. When did this begin to happen? I believe it began when we older neighbours began to let go of our distress at the changes and started to remember. Remember what? The tradition of neighbourliness in our corner of Elbow Park that goes back nearly one hundred years. In that light, we recalled the words of Al, retired architect, former president of the local historical society, on the eve of his departure from our street. In essence, he told us, "Remember to tell the new people that come here stories about the legacy of this neighbourly community. They will want to know."

So it is coming to pass. For example, we older ones have been approached when the bell-ringers are practicing: "Tell us about the bells; our children are intrigued and they want to go inside the church. Would that be all right?" One day one of our neighbours commented, "I didn't know that your husband was a minister until the people next door told me. Lately, I've been thinking I would like to speak to him because I'm concerned about our children's future. In such a troubled society as we have today, I want them to experience growth in their spirits."

John was glad to listen to her and soon at her request, he lent her a selection of little books of Bible stories for young children. Her young son chose one, sat down and immediately began to read while his younger sister examined the pictures closely. Now, we are hearing from other new neighbours of their interest in forming Adult Bible study groups, just as those of us experienced when we were their age. Story telling, the heart of community, is not dead.

MORE THAN A TENDRIL OF HOPE...

A Community of Strangers

In the light of these thoughts, I was in for an encouraging surprise while visiting Montreal this spring. John and I found ourselves attending quite by chance a gathering of the Montreal Storyteller's Guild at the Atwater Library. The leader of the Guild told me when I phoned, "Please come. Quite a number of our regulars are attending a festival of story telling in Toronto, so we might be a bit thin on the ground."

We arrived to discover the chairs set in a circle and, significantly, a large lighted candle set high, symbolic, I thought, of the gathering of the community around the fire. Indeed, while at first there were only about six people, before we were to begin, over twenty had settled in. I discovered upon our arrival that story telling to the Montreal Guild is expressed literally in the telling, not in this case, in the reading. And soon both John and I found ourselves on the roster that evening!

Spinning Tales in the City

Not unlike my own approach to writing memoirs, the leader led off with a personal story from her childhood. Her memories were of the old Victorian house her parents had bought for $15,000, before the Great Depression hit hard, in a small town not far from Chicago. There was an overgrown but spacious area where her mother could at last fulfill her desire to garden. Stretching beyond the back fence were the unthreatening woods where she and the neighbourhood children could safely play. Ultimately, she and her friends would reach young adulthood together. I was enchanted by her story and by the intense listening to each other as the evening progressed.

John told a personal story of a compassionate man he knew, Henry, who shared what little he had with others in need of a helping hand. He was compassionate toward his team of horses after hauling hay in the hot, humid summer, unharnessing them immediately and leading them to drink from the cool stream flowing through his field. He treated them well not only because without them he couldn't earn a living, but because they were God's creatures. When one unpopular, troublesome resident of the village was in need, Henry applied the same attitude toward him. In time, the man responded by helping Henry, not by coercion but by example.

When my turn came, I told of an experience John and I had in following a circular path in the mystic Roseland peninsula of Cornwall, England. On the way we met a woman who could communicate with the creatures ~ for example, a blackbird (Cornish thrush) that followed her around her garden, and a seal in the harbour who hurried to see her when she called. Even the pansies growing in boxes on a stone wall followed her. But that's another story!

When the story telling ended, people stood up and turned to speak to one another. A long-haired young man with a big pack on his back approached us. Turning to John, he said, "I was moved by your story about Henry's sensitivity to nature, animals and people, and the response it engenders. There is a musical term that can be applied to this kind of sensitivity where a resonance occurs, as between the various instruments being played in a group, but also among the players. It's called 'entrainment'." He continued, "This evening we've been experiencing entrainment between the teller, bringing to life a story, and the listener, caught up in the telling."

John and I were intrigued by the young man's enlightenment and as we looked around at those gathered there, we were encouraged by the obvious interaction among the several generations present, an encouraging sign of urban community in the making. Perhaps this kind of connection with others can be the antidote to what Thomas Merton described as a society "concerned only with 'practicality' ~ 'efficiency,' that is, with means not ends ... having lost our ability to see life whole."

Some time later, I looked up in the French dictionary the meaning of '*entraînement*'. First, *entrain:* liveliness, spirit, life; *entraînement:* attraction, involvement; and then, *entraînement d'une mélodie:* being carried along or carried away by music. Indeed, the young man was right; entrainment is what the evening with the story tellers and listeners was all about.

I believe that, currently, this urban rediscovery of the ancient art of story telling is an encouraging attempt to 'grow community' in spite of the rapid expansion of cities and the fast pace of life it creates. For the stories we shared that evening did not really begin until the tall candle was lit and we had formed a circle in the middle of the room. As we told our stories and listened to those of the others, we became part of that community. What we experienced, therefore, offers hope in a world marked by restlessness, hopelessness and a sense of inevitable danger.

EXPERIENCING COMMUNITY IN TRAVEL

Learning to 'Bide a While'

For a tourist, there is great delight in travelling through a country one is visiting for the first time. The various landscapes unfold swiftly with a turn in the road, the rise to a hill, the descent to a valley. The approach of a village near the sea, a distant town embraced by a river, the anticipation of a city, rising from a plain, all recall the delight of the child, turning the bright pages of a picture book. But after a while, I begin to wonder, Who lives here? What is it like to live here?

John and I decided that being merely a tourist can become a lonely pursuit. So in subsequent travels to Ireland, we began to slow down, seeking to meet the strangers whose communities we had entered. We began to rent what is called 'self-catering accommodation' ~ a little cottage where we could look after ourselves and still become a part of the community. Someplace where we could 'bide a while.'

Initially, our conversations with people we met were casual and brief: a chance meeting by the sea with a young man and his beautiful Doberman who had only three legs. The young man was amazed that the dog took to us right away. "My dog," he remarked, "knows everyone in the village. You're strangers to him, yet he obviously likes you!"

On another occasion while climbing a hill, we met a farmer and his border collie. The dog approached as if he had known us all along. "Ah," the farmer said, "he is a kind dog." We nodded, recalling the many years of our own 'kind' dogs. (Friendly dogs, in their way, introduce their masters, not the other way round.)

But as we made the transition from being tourists, we found that renting accommodation from owners who lived nearby drew us closer to the heart of communities.

Portscatho-Gerrans, Cornwall, UK

The very first Celtic land John and I visited was Cornwall, England, in 1962. I credit the travel writer, H.V. Morton, and his book, *In Search of England*, for my early interest. It was first published in 1927, the year I was born. When I was a young woman, I found a rather battered copy in a second-hand bookstore and literally began to pore over it. I read voraciously his stories covering one end of England to the other. But it was the fourth chapter that charmed me by the very first line of its little preface: "I fall in love with Cornwall and with a name." And that name was St. Anthony of Roseland.

St. Anthony lies within the context of villages named for Celtic saints. It is just as H.V. Morton writes,

> Here the saints have taken root like white daisies in a field. Is there a saintlier country on earth? St. Austell, St. Anthony, St. Mawes, and St. Ives; St. Agnes, St. Neot, St. Pinnock, and St.

Mellion; St. Germans, St. Breock, St. Eval, and St. Columb - - they ring like a peal of bells over a meadow. And what strange saints! Cornwall was converted by the Celtic church, and England by the Romans. These names preserved on the map of Cornwall, are those of holy men [and women] from Wales and Ireland who, when the legions were recalled and England became a wild battleground of men and gods, guarded Christ in the mountains.

Since childhood I have known that many villages in Quebec are named for saints, especially those that lie within the region I have passed through many a time on the way to my own old village, Inverness, Megantic County. To this day their names ring in my ears: St-Hyacinthe, St-Wenceslas, Ste-Eulalie, Ste-Marie, and Ste-Anastasie, St-Georges-de-Beauce, St-Pierre-Baptiste, St-Jean-de-Brébeuf. When I look at Morton's list, I note the English abbreviation for Saint, 'St.,' which doesn't indicate the gender of the saints, unlike the Romance language, French.

Going as far back as childhood, I was certainly accustomed to the sounds of their names, like a peal of bells in my ears, but, equally, I delighted in sounding them, feeling them on my tongue. Later, as I understood the importance in French of the distinct designations for masculine and feminine, I could imagine those saintly folk, men and women following their holy lives. Then would come the turn up into the Appalachian hills, the hills of home, the sign reading 'Inverness' and just a little further on, 'Lower Ireland' (now St-Jean-de-Brébeuf, a Canadian saint), the sign a glimpse of the history of Celtic settlement in my old community.

Ah, but the name 'St. Anthony in Roseland' and its companion village, 'St. Just in Roseland', long ago captured me. But it was not until 1995 that we visited that part of Cornwall, the Roseland peninsula, which looks out to the Atlantic shipping lanes. We stayed in a house halfway up the hill between two villages immediately adjacent to one another, just a few miles away from St. Anthony and St. Just. The name was Portscatho-Gerrans, rather than saints' names. The hyphenated name is both picturesque and of a story-telling nature. Portscatho means a gathering place of little boats and Gerrans is associated with the tales of King Arthur of the Round Table. As the vicar of St. Just in Roseland tells Morton:

> [St. Just] ... was Jestyn, son of Geraint ... of the Round Table. ...the legend is that when he died he was borne across the bay at Gerrans, just at the back there, in a golden boat with silver oars, and buried beneath Carne Beacon.

Every morning at breakfast we looked out at that storied bay and every evening watched for the little lights on the buoys to come on. And during the day we walked along the coastal path, gazing at the ebb and flow of the sea and looking up as the skylark made his spiraling ascent into the blue. Now and again, my imagination was touched by the romance of the old tales. But sad to say, the reality of the little fishing boats in the port of Portscatho was that their absence, the result of international overfishing in the 1990s that was being borne in upon all fisherman, made them conspicuous.

VE Day Celebration

On this visit to Cornwall, our two friends, Hank and Dorothy Floyd, former Verdunites like ourselves, accompanied us. We enjoyed accompanying them to the church where in the 18th century two of Hank's ancestors had been married. A few days later we invited them to come with us to the village of Marazion from where, if the tide was out, we could walk on a cobble stone walkway across the bay to St. Michael's Mount and the castle built high upon it. Indeed, the tide was out so over we went, walking on the bottom of the sea! On the return trip, we were rowed over the waves to shore in a sturdy boat.

One morning, Ingelore Radford, our host in Portscatho-Gerrans, reminded us of Saturday's events. "The first event," she hastened to tell us, "is that all the children will be served their tea by the adults and each will be given a commemorative mug as a me-

mento of this special day." The children were to be served in this manner for two reasons, I thought. Surely, it can be said, that the younger generations owe much to the old generation who fought in World War II. The children's response was emphatic, judging by the displays of red, white and blue posters they had made and placed in shop windows all along the main street. "Thank you, Senior Citizens," came through loud and clear.

It was the two older generations ~ paents and grandparents ~ I saw serving the children. This reflected the second thought ~ we older ones bear toward the children a heavy responsibility: to work for peace so that they might not suffer the despair and devastation of war. So remembering and serving went hand in hand on that Saturday.

Before the children sat down to eat, the local band accompanied the school choirs in such tunes as 'There'll Always Be an England', 'Eidelweiss' and 'Wish Me Luck as You Wave Me Goodbye'. Wearing red, white and blue paper party hats, the children sat at long tables decorated with the Union Jack and the Cornish flag. Their heads kept bobbing up and down to the music of the band. Yet, every now and again, a solemn expression would pass over their faces.

When the children were well launched into their tea, the senior citizens sat down at little tables nearby to be served by the middle generation. Ingelore introduced us to the others and soon we were engaged in conversation almost as if we were permanent residents. Before long, John and I entered into a spirited conversation with the Church of England parish priest, the Reverend Diane Powell. She was, perhaps in her early fifties, a Devon 'lass' who had worked as a town clerk before undertaking theological studies. She had a smiling face, a direct gaze and obviously enjoyed her role and service in that community.

We discovered her lively interest in the Celtic saints of old, whose reputation as holy men and women abounds in Cornwall ~ an ancient stronghold of Celtic spirituality. Diane informed us of the signs of a revival of interest in the legacy of the saints and what is significant, an ecumenical and international expression of it taking place.

In the sixth century these saints traveled to France from England, Scotland, Ireland, and Wales. Today, pilgrimages and retreats are taking place, Diane told us, as people express a longing for growth in their spirits. Indeed, she is one of the leaders of this movement. We find this especially good news, as we paused with these dear Cornish folk to remember the deep sacrifice for peace, only fifty years ago.

As I think of that afternoon's activities, the image of children solemnly eating cake, frosted in red, white and blue, and served by their elders, melds with the image of the saints who walked this land, crossing the channel to take the Good News of the Prince of Peace.

"The second event," Ingelore reminded us, "is the Victory dance this evening in the Portscatho Social Club ~ live music, too!" That evening Hank, Dorothy and John and I walked down the hill with much anticipation, for the posters in the villages had been announcing all week that Patsy MacLean and Paul Vincent would be entertaining us with music and songs from the 1940s. So there would be not only dancing, but also a singalong.

We were greeted at the door by a smiling, grey-haired woman. When we introduced ourselves as visitors from Canada, we were met with such warmth that the others turned to look. In a moment we knew why. We were no sooner seated at a table across the room, when a middle-aged, sandy-haired man with a ruddy face came striding purposefully over to us. "Are we glad to see you Canadians! I'm a fisherman; I've been fishing for over twenty-two years and I can tell you Canadians that you're heroes as far as all of us are concerned."

He went on to give his reasons for such a declaration. A number of European fisher-groups had, for quite some time, firsthand experience of overfishing by the Spanish fleets. This Cornishman was expressing the local dissatisfaction with lack of action by the European Union against such fishing practices. Brian Tobin, from

Newfoundland and our Canadian minister of fisheries at that time, had tackled this long-simmering problem while ministers from other countries had dragged their feet. As far as this Cornish fisherman was concerned, Tobin had done a favour to many aggrieved people in the fishing industry.

It was obvious to us that this part of the programme was devoted to an integral part of village life, the simple joy of getting together, relaxing with a drink and, in this case, making welcome the visiting Canadians. As a matter of fact, during our time in Portscatho-Gerrans, we came across no other Canadians.

At one point, the publican of the Social Club crossed the room from the bar to a television mounted high enough for all to see and turned it on. Suddenly we found ourselves in Hyde Park, London. Actor Robert Hardy, familiar as Siegfried Farnon, a veterinarian in James Herriot's *All Creatures Great and Small*, was the master of ceremonies on this 50th anniversary of VE Day. He spoke using Winston Churchill's words, his voice resonating in the familiar accents of Churchill's speech.

The Queen and the Royal Family members along with thousands upon thousands of people listened intently, even as all of us gathered there in the Social Club. After two minutes of silence, there in Portscatho-Gerrans, we joined in remembering England's great sacrifice for peace, and also, that of her Allies. The silence was broken by hearty singing of 'There'll Always Be an England', as many a tear was wiped away.

It was time now for the dancing and singing to begin. Patsy MacLean began to sing to Paul Vincent's accompaniment. Her voice was strong, throaty and melodious. He played on a keyboard connected to a synthesizer so his music approached the Big Band sound so familiar to us all. Mostly the crowd was late middle-age, our youth going back to the '40s, but by no means was the crowd looking for slow-only waltz numbers!

As John and I joined the dancers, we glanced across the room at Hank and Dot who kept perfect time to the jitterbug beat of our youth. Soon we were caught up in the joy of a room full of seniors giving themselves over to the familiar lively music, our faces smiling almost like children at play. Later, our only complaint was that Glenn Miller's 'In the Mood' was delivered at half the speed that we were brought up on!

At about ten o'clock a buffet was laid out on long tables. There were sandwiches plump with fresh crab, which our fisherman friend informed us he had caught. There were plates of rich Cornish delicacies ~ great round layer cakes in white and chocolate and decorated with coloured frostings. There were fruity tarts, and nutty cookies. And, of course, steaming cups of good, strong tea.

The party was beginning to wind down. We had enjoyed a full day. As we moved toward the door, voices called us. It was the woman who had first greeted us and beside her stood the fisherman who, indeed, was her son. We heard, "We're so glad you came," and then they both embraced us. Her son had the last word. "As soon as you can, get over to the harbour at St. Mawes and you'll see Canadian flags flying from the masts alongside the black and white Cornish flag of St. Perrin."

As we opened the door to step into the night, we were suddenly taken aback by the clapping of hands as the people smiled and nodded at us. Oh, Canada, I thought, the Old Country not only recognizes you but is giving you a salute!

The next day, John and I traveled over to St. Mawes, St. Anthony and St. Just, and there, offshore from the Roseland villages, we saw the fishing boats that were under way flying the Canadian maple-leaf flag alongside the Cornish flag. According to custom, when the boats were anchored the flags were lowered. On our return we drove inland to see our flag hoisted up tall flag poles in many a garden as well as smaller ones placed in front windows. In all our travels we had never seen such a sight.

John entering woods to see the Gleanies

Fishing boats in harbour

Cornwall 1995

Passing on Gratitude

A few years ago, Brian Tobin, no longer in government, visited Calgary to promote a book he had written about his time on Parliament Hill. Of course, it includes reference to his initiative in addressing the growing problem of overfishing. During the question period, John and I stood up. "We haven't any questions but we want you to know that in 1995 we were in the Roseland peninsula area of Cornwall." And then we conveyed the gratitude expressed by the Cornish fishing fraternity toward him and Canada. Tobin looked both surprised and pleased, striding over to where we stood to shake our hands. "I see," he said, "that I have a couple of friends here!" Both John and I were satisfied that we had delivered a vote of thanks on behalf of the Cornish folk we had met, even though it was somewhat late.

The Circular Path

Ingelore had given us a pamphlet on the circular paths of the Portscatho-Gerrans area. By mid-morning we set off with a snack of buttered brown bread, a chunk of cheese, a couple of slices of John's chocolate cake, digestive biscuits, two little cartons of yoghurt, a bottle of orange juice, one of water, and two ripe pears. We were not going to be feeling 'pinched'!

We headed out on the public footpath at the end of the little cul-de-sac where we were staying. On either side, high hedges, rooted on ancient stone walls, hummed with the sound of bees. The flowering shrubs and wild flowers blanketed the wall with their growth. As we strode along toward the village of Gerrans, a multi-scented profusion of bluebells, white campion, yellow buttercups, and blue and yellow forget-me-nots brightened out way. In a few minutes we had reached the village. The directions in the pamphlet told us to take the path near the garage that would lead us to a circular path heading toward the fields of Lanhay, the very name having a mystical tone.

After a false start, we returned to the garage owner's home and enquired of his wife how to get onto the circular path. "Just a minute," she said, as she put the dog inside the house. Without a word, she set off down the sidewalk to the corner, humming a little tune to "diddly dum ti dum," as we followed. She waved to us as we set out more confidently.

We were about to climb the wooden stile when we noticed a Canadian flag in the window of the nearby farmhouse. I stuck my head through the gateway and saw a man bending over a spread of purple, yellow and white pansies growing through the gravel of the driveway. I called out to him, "We're stopping to salute the flag and to shake the hand of the Cornishman who put it there!" He straightened up and smiled at us immediately. "Are you Canadians?" he asked. When we assured him we were, he called his wife who was in the doorway of the house.

What followed was a stimulating conversation that started with statements of political content in a range of opinions about the European Union, the Canadian federation, Canadian action against Spanish overfishing, and national identity. It went on to the wonder of pansies that refused to be confined only to boxes mounted on a stone wall. Sending their seeds on the wind to find root in the gravel below, they bloomed year after year in spite of being walked on and driven over.

This phenomenon of nature was followed by another, even more astounding one. While we talked, a blackbird lighted on the stone wall. "Oh," the man said to his wife, "there's your bird come for a snack." She turned to the corner of the doorstep and reached into a bucket on the step. The bird immediately flew toward her and settled where she knelt to watch him. John and I were entranced.

As the bird fed, the man explained that his wife had made friends with the creature about three years ago. It had not been the case of a bird brought back to health by the careful ministrations of a human. As the woman told us, "This one among all the others who pass by, had approached me directly. It goes about with the other birds, but it is the only one who will drop by to visit like this. When I'm gardening and using the wheelbarrow, it will light on the barrow and ride along while I'm pushing it." I found this such a touching story. "It's a gift you have!" I said. She smiled at me and nodded. "Just like St. Francis," I added and she nodded again.

While John and her husband talked in the driveway, Mrs. Raven, as was her marvelously appropriate name, invited me inside to see their house. It was a long, rectangular, two-storey stone building, set amid sloping fields of about thirty-five acres. "It used to be an old barn, built over a hundred years ago," she told me. As I followed her from one bright room to another, she would point out what part of the barn this and that area represented ~ the stables, the sheep pen and finally the abattoir "where," she said, "the bullocks stood waiting to be slaughtered."

The whole interior space had been transformed into a welcoming, comfortable home with large windows looking out upon green fields, stone walls and sky-scapes arching over an extent of the Roseland peninsula as far as the eye could see. The ambiance had been transformed by a melding of design and execution to create this house out of a barn. She, a native Cornish woman, and her husband, a Gloucestershire man who retired from a military career in the British Air Force and was a veteran of World War II, had together made a home out of a barn; that's a fact. But I did not doubt that the woman's spirit of empathy with creatures was behind the transformation.

We bade goodbye to the Ravens and headed back onto the circular path. The sun was climbing higher into the sky even as the path wound its way through the green Fields of Lanhay to hills ascending to the height of land and a gravel road. A farmer, come to tend to his fences, nodded at us as we climbed the stile to the road. Following the pamphlet's directions, we turned left as the road descended. Soon there appeared on our right a gracious white, gabled house with a forget-me-not blue door and window frames; the voices of children drifted from somewhere beyond the hedges.

The house was situated on a rise, opening almost a direct perspective onto the tidal area we hoped to cross. The thought came to me, What a natural way to observe the marking of time through the ebb and flow of the tides acting upon the sea's little tributary, the Polingey creek! We shifted our gaze toward it, remembering the words of the garageman's wife. "If the tide is out you'll be able to cross on stepping-stones laid out to the other side." Soon we could detect the acrid iodine smell of seaweed, which grew stronger as we followed down a little path.

We drew closer. Old stepping-stones, laid long ago, made a path through the seaweed and wet tidal mud. We paused; to our right, fishing boats and launches listed where they had come to rest as the tide had receded. On the opposite shore, not a human voice could be heard in the late morning air but blackbirds whistled, "Argee-bargee," interspersed with their sweetly tuneful notes. Indeed, all nature appeared to be singing ~ bees in the banks of bluebells and warblers overhead in the high hedges, shaking the bushes and the air with tumbling notes.

We set foot in the creek bed in the manner of inlanders, not at all sure that the tide wouldn't suddenly rush toward us. Perhaps, the familiar saying, 'Time and Tide Wait for No Man', was at the back of our minds! But the stepping-stones were firm beneath our feet and we did not slip. We entered the path enclosed by a steeply rising field on our right and on our left, thickets bordering the creek; indeed, in sections of it we were progressing through a winding green tunnel rather than walking on a path. There we sat down, eating our lunch hungrily before setting out for the last lap of the circular path.

Soon we came to a stile at the bottom of a steep stretch. Suddenly, a cacophony of sounds filled the air ~ the sharp, staccato sound of birds low to the ground. Immediately, John's reaction was to imitate their sound; after a pause, an even more feverish outbreak was heard from the birds. Almost simultaneously, dogs burst into frantic barking, followed by a woman speaking sharply to them. We climbed the stile and swung around to see two women and two dogs on the other side of a little gate. Beyond the gate, a gently sloping lawn was visible with flowering shrubs, beds of spring flowers and young trees interspersed among old ones, bordering the grassy place.

We exchanged greetings, and after a moment of sizing us up, one of the women opened the gate and invited us in. "What kind of birds did we just hear?" John asked. "Come over this way and see," she replied, motioning toward the bottom of the slope.

There a flock of about a dozen guinea birds moved nervously hither and thither as one. "They don't know you," the woman who had admitted us remarked. Obviously they felt at home with the two women and the dogs, and as long as we stood quietly some distance from them, the birds continued to glean the turf.

It became apparent to us that this green expanse of tended grass and cultivated arboretum and garden belonged to the woman who had let us in. Her little border collie had an attitude of a guardian toward the birds, as did the woman. Her friend sat on a blanket holding the leash of a black labrador, now patient and calm beside her.

We were told that the birds live in the wild and their species has been in the area a very long time. The local Cornish people call them the 'gleanies' because, indeed, they glean for their food. "A fox lives not far away," the woman told us, "but the birds roost in the trees, which is in their favour." She went on, "They are very brave and also very foolish." Our host told us of observing them, at the moment they had spotted a fox lurking about. They mustered their forces and advanced as one in a straight line toward the fox, all the time clacketing in their incessant staccato. In essence, they unnerved him so that he turned tail and slunk away.

However, we were informed they don't make good parents, for they drop their eggs here and there, appearing to forget where their nests are. When they do manage to sit long enough for the chicks to hatch, they will wander off. Then suddenly they seem to recall that somewhere there must be a baby or two and will begin to frantically search until they find them. Yet, in spite of all this apparent carelessness, the guinea birds continue to survive in Cornwall.

Before we left her place, Mrs. Tilton, as was her name, told us that she and Mrs. Raven are friends. She smiled and said, "Indeed, she does have the gift of being able to communicate with creatures." Then she went on to tell us that her friend calls to the seals in Gerrans' Bay, "and one of them out of all the others, comes close to shore where she stands. As she speaks to the animal it responds in its own voice." Her friend sighed. "I wish I had the gift, too," she said softly. "So do I," I replied.

As we left to complete the last of the circular path, we hoped to catch a glimpse of Mrs. Tilton's house. We passed more arboretums and developed ponds where swans glided gracefully, but no house was to be seen. A day or two later our hosts, Ingelore and Roy Radford, told us that Mr. and Mrs. Tilton, who have developed the lovely area we had entered, don't have their house there. They live in the village, but choose to cultivate and enjoy their property, their own private park, as a place of retreat. We realized then what a privilege Mrs. Tilton had accorded us two Canadian visitors by inviting us in to share for a few moments the beauty of the place where the gleanies are at home.

Indeed, the circular path had brought us in a circle in more ways than one. Mrs. Raven's gift was further corroborated just as we came to the point where the circular path opened up to where we had begun, behind the Gerrans' garage. John and I will always remember these Cornish folk, their appreciation of nature, their cultivation of green and splendid spaces and empathy with the creatures who cohabit the earth, even in the nearby sea. Our walk that day has reminded me of a saying reflective of Celtic thought by Martin Wallace of St. Peter's Chapel, Bradwell-on-Sea ~ a small Celtic church on the coast of Essex, built by St. Cedd of Lindisfarne in 654 A.D.: "Let God speak to you through creation, and so carry you with the tides and the season, the current and the waves."

Mrs. Raven and frind

John on the river bed

NORTHERN IRELAND:
THE ROAD IS A'TURNING

A Bend in the Road for Us

At Christmas in 2003, there was no greeting card from Wilma. I've written about our dear Northern Irish friend in *The Spiral Road* and the friendship we have shared since 1979. Something had to be wrong. We let the phone ring several times until she answered in a thin, quavering voice, the words hesitating between long pauses.

"I ~ can't ~ speak...," she muttered.

"Have you had a stroke?" I asked.

"Yes."

"Do your arms and legs work?"

"Yes. I ~ can't ~ speak," she repeated.

"Oh, Wilma," John and I said. "So sorry, so sorry." Then, as she has often declared before, "I – love – you ~ both." We answered, "Oh, we love you, too."

We were aware that during the last few visits, Wilma would say, "I'm not what I was," and John and I would nod and say, "Neither are we." Then we'd smile at each other, acknowledging that "the spirit is willing, but the flesh is weak." Our last Irish visit was in 2000. John had been diagnosed with prostate cancer in June of 2003. Nevertheless, he is afforded a good quality of life thanks to important research culminating in promising medications. I take medication for a cardiac condition that has been stable for nearly twenty years. Thus, like many seniors, we are the beneficiaries of advanced knowledge and treatment of ailments that our parents could not have imagined. So our thinking, following our telephone conversation with Wilma, was how could we *not* go again to Northern Ireland for our dear friend's sake?

By February, 2004, John, the 'travel agent', had found us a traditional Irish cottage in the foothills of the Sperrin mountains in County Tyrone, only about twelve miles from Wilma's home.

It had been several years since Wilma had ended her Farm Bed and Breakfast undertaking, known widely for her warmth and generous hospitality. In April of 2000, we had spent ten days with her. "Your bed is all ready," she had declared, "with the beautiful rose and blue quilt you sent me from Quebec." Without a doubt, the significance of that quilt, made in the Gatineau valley of Quebec, where so many Irish had emigrated during the Potato Famine, was appreciated by Wilma to receive and for us to give.

However, in March 2004 John underwent cataract surgery in both eyes, and as it turned out, the left eye was slower to recover. Before the end of April, John suggested that we find a family member who could accompany us during the first part of our trip. It happened that our son Tom (for ten days) and our grown granddaughter, Sarah, (for a week) were able to come. For both of them, although they had been with us in Ireland in 1997, this would be their first occasion to explore the Antrim coast, where it is believed my father's ancestors, by the name of Canning, originated.

But now for the first time, Wilma would not be showing us to our room with the beautiful quilt. While she was able to still live in her home with regular help of family and other caregivers, her days of offering hospitality to friends had come to an end. We were to discover how deeply that loss was already affecting her.

As soon as we were settled in our rented traditional cottage, we phoned Wilma to tell her that we, along with Tom and Sarah, whom she knew, were ready to come to see her. "Oh, I'm not ready yet for you ~ come in a couple of days." So it was settled, we thought, that we would go for tea in the afternoon. However when we arrived, Wilma commented that John and I would be sleeping under that beautiful quilt again. Only then did we realize how her mind appeared to be unsettled. While her memory was sharp enough to still experience our mutual friendship, she could not understand why we had not come to stay with her as in the past.

Jean, a friend of Wilma, went into the kitchen to prepare the tea for the six of us. With her went Sarah, who Wilma once said reminded her of her own daughters when they were Sarah's age.

Almost immediately Wilma became agitated, rushing into the kitchen to reclaim her place as host to her guests. Jean spoke to her calmly, encouraging her to return to the living room where we were waiting. It was an emotional afternoon for all of us. Yet, as we returned several times during our stay last spring, Wilma appeared to understand that we were not far away and that we were looking after ourselves.

One afternoon she said, "I'm - so - alone," in spite of the good care that surrounded her. I thought of my father who suffered a stroke at the age of sixty-six. To have one's power of speech or movement diminished so swiftly must be a crushing blow. My father remained paralyzed on his left side. In time he regained his facility of speech, yet for quite a long time, his emotions seemed jumbled ~ he would cry when he meant to laugh and laugh when he was sad.

When his power of concentration eventually improved so that he could enjoy reading again, he began to be able to rely on his expression of emotions. However, in the early aftermath of his stroke, he was as someone bereft like Wilma. Perhaps, the cry, "I'm so alone," uttered by the stroke victim means, "For it is myself I have lost."

One day shortly before our departure for home, Wilma's sister, Rosanna, described an image her sister's doctor had used regarding the confusion caused by the stroke. "It's as if the mind has become like a book whose pages have loosened. Every time the book is opened the pages flutter out in no orderly manner. That's how Wilma's thoughts and emotions are expressed, and, of course, that exaggerates her behaviour."

On our last visit with our friend, there was a moment when we stood together at her door. "I'm - so - alone," she repeated.

The three of us joined hands. For twenty-seven years, we kept a deep and long friendship, in spite of visits only every three or four years or so. John reminded Wilma of the prayers she had asked him to compose for her, once in her home four years ago and once when we had phoned her one Christmas.

Road to Antrim Coast

Sarah on the Antrim Coast

She nodded thoughtfully. John asked, "Would you like me to say a prayer for you now?" "Yes," Wilma replied. And John prayed, his voice full of emotion, for Wilma to experience peace in her heart from the One whom she has always known who created her as a woman of warm heart, full of kindness, generosity, and constancy in friendship. "You know we came to Northern Ireland to see you when we heard you weren't well because we love you," I said. "I know," Wilma replied. God be with you, dear friend, until we meet again, I thought.

Still Moments Observed: Tom
On his first visit to the Antrim coast, Tom walked over to an opening in a high hedge, overlooking the sea. There he stood, motionless, his feet firmly planted, hands by his side, back straight, head raised high, totally absorbed in gazing at the sea, blue as the sky above. And all the while, the waves rose and fell to slide forward and back upon the beach as if in greeting.

Moments passed and still Tom stood, his attitude of one listening intently to a communication from Nature. Perhaps, even, this setting from which his ancestors sailed to Quebec nearly two hundred years ago, gave him some sense of their spirits. I did not ask, for those still moments were his.

Tom's Walk on Antrim Beach
Every now and again, Tom interrupts his walk on the smooth, brown beach to suddenly bend here and there to gaze at the colourful plethora of tiny stones spread widely and lavishly for all to see. Above, the sun and clouds in playful mood alternately shed light and shadow upon the stones ~ opaque, smooth and white, mottled with brown specks, translucent quartz, green, bluish and nearly mauve ~ like field, sea and sky. Some resemble a tiny bird's egg, a heart, a moon, even a tiny bog-land, all shaped by collaboration of sea and shore.

Bending again and again, totally absorbed, he makes his selection. As we approach from our walk, he wordlessly opens his hands to show us his treasure. Later, in our Tyrone cottage, we catch through the open door of his room, a glimpse of his treasure, placed with delicate care in a small open box lined with tissue paper. These are gifts for his loved ones from Irish Nature and Tom.

Sarah's Nook

In the morning after our arrival at our rented traditional Irish cottage, Sarah was sound asleep in the 'cultyee,' set in the corner of the kitchen. It serves as a seat during the day and a bed by night, backed by a little window that frames a corner of the evergreen trees and a patch of sky above. Snug as could be with an extra mattress from a folding bed, Sarah was nestled deep in a generous, flowery duvet. As I put the water on for tea and porridge, I heard, "Good morning, Grandma," delivered in a sleepy yet 'comfy' tone.

Her bed lay between the peat-burning fireplace and the wall with its little window. At night, when the rest of us had retired, Sarah would drift to sleep near the glow of the quiet peat flames on her left and the still darkness on her right, lighted by stars shining through the branches. In the early morning the birds of spring would sing to greet the dawn. All of this restfulness, I believe, contributed to her peaceful awakening that morning. Her friends and colleagues at home exclaimed, as she later reported to us, "Sarah, you look fantastic and you were in Ireland only one week!"

Sarah in Jet Lag

Sarah, still a little jet lagged, rides in the back seat beside me; in the front are our son Tom ~ the driver, and John ~ the guide. We pass through valleys, brilliant with April green, rising to meet the fertile fields of the Sperrin Mountain foothills, even as the road we follow rises to meet us. "It is all so beautiful," she murmurs. There is a pause and I remark, "Remember those beautiful blonde Connamara beaches on our visit seven years ago?" No answer. Sarah is suddenly fast asleep. She lets out a long sigh and soon her head comes to rest on my shoulder.

Later, when she wakens, I hear, "Oh, I'm sorry; what were you saying?" I reply, "It doesn't matter. Take your rest." She puts her head down again for a few minutes. This time it is I who sigh ~ this grandmother in old age, sitting next to Sarah, a young woman greatly in need of a little holiday, and sharing it with us.

Unlikely Neighbours

Our little Irish cottage is set in a 'clachan,' a cluster of neighbouring cottages, reached by a winding path overlooking a little valley just down from the Creagen Visitor Centre. Each cottage is named for one of the prehistoric standing stones and circles that abound in the area. 'Tornoge' accommodated the four of us, and after Tom and Sarah left, we stayed in 'Cregnavesky,' with a bedroom upstairs, which we are accustomed to.

The Visitor Centre is known for its diverse facilities. There is a photo display and history of nearby ancient stones, standing erect and in circles, complete with information about guided walks and tours. As well, there are theatres suitable for musical events and productions by regional filmmakers and story tellers. The gift shop has great drawing power ~ a celebration of the work of local artists: sparkling silver rings, brooches and pendants, adorned with amethysts, garnets, moonstones and other semiprecious stones, and always in a setting of spiral swirls.

The colourful pottery dazzles the eyes. The shifting rainbow colours of raku and the shining smoothness of rounded bowls in natural colours invite you to stroke them. Paintings on wood, in earthen colours, reflect the deep layers of earth the prehistoric stones have rested upon, while here there is the suggestion of humanoids, long gone and curled in the fetal position amid fragments of spiral swirls.

And that is not all. There are locations suitable for business conventions, drawing upon European Union clientele as well as for gatherings that represent the local people's interests. To top it off, there is an excellent restaurant, hosting a variety of occasions, including weddings, anniversaries, meals for schoolchildren and their teachers who arrive in busloads to explore the surrounding area, and even family celebrations of their children's First Communion on Pentecost Day.

The centre is built on level ground. On one side, there is a beautiful brown bog-land, arrayed with flashes of colourful spring flora and vibrant with the call of birds. On the other, a stand of evergreen trees overlooks a spacious courtyard. Up and down the narrow lanes, banks of bluebells, white anemones and tiny white Michaelmas daisies, traced with pink, express their glory and lend their fragrance to the soft spring air. Overhead tumble the flute-like notes of Irish blackbirds, the trills of robins and blue-trimmed flycatchers. The building, built of local dark grey stone, rises from the ground to a sloping roof, higher in the back than in the front. It faces a courtyard and is backed by a pond, home to a pair of big white ducks that bob their heads in greeting the passersby on the path.

One night just after we had gone to bed, the sound of motorcycles traveling on the nearby road began to grow in intensity. Soon we realized that they had turned into the laneway leading to the clachan where our cottage was located. We rose to look out the upstairs window and then realized we were about to have new neighbours in two unoccupied cottages, while their companions were heading to other cottages in nearby clachans.

Of course, we were curious about them, especially when we began to hear the bikers speaking quietly together, some in English and some in French. Obviously, they were trying not to disturb us. Soon they entered their cottages and shortly all was quiet. The next day, Marianne, a young Englishwoman, said, "We arrived late and were trying not to disturb you. After all, we didn't want you to think we were the Hell's Angels!"

45

In the week that followed, the story of who they were and why they traveled together gradually unfolded. Most importantly, the reason behind their association, we believe, gives hope to the world. Somewhere along the way, each national group had moved from focusing entirely on fellow bikers from their own country to acknowledging a wider fraternity. In this case, it was an Anglo-France/France-Anglo association of bikers. One of them, Barry, a British businessman declared, "We have among our group a top auto mechanic and a top accountant for a multi-billion-dollar company."

And again, Marianne told us, "Many of the French group are Parisian motorcycle policemen, men and women. Several years ago some of us decided to approach the French bikers' association to see if they would like to join us on a trip on the continent. We all arranged to take our holiday at the same time so we could travel together. When we did our first trip, I looked across the restaurant where we'd stopped for a break and saw that on one side we English had begun to eat together and on the other side, likewise, the French." Marianne continued, "This won't do, I thought. So now we've been sitting together, and we are actually gaining confidence in each other's language. It seems the right way to go these days."

The age span among these people was, perhaps, mid-thirties to the fifties. This particular spring Ireland was the chosen country to visit, mainly Northern Ireland, Donegal and Galway, all places John and I have visited since 1979. In the evening when they returned they would tell us where they had been, of the music they had heard and of the breathtaking, diverse beauty of Ireland they had passed through.

One evening I was walking back along the path from the Centre to our cottage when I caught up with three of the French women. I asked, "Où étiez-vous aujourd'hui?" One of them replied, "La côte d'Antrim." "Quelle place?" I countered. In a rush of words, she began to speak too quickly for my ear ... something about Derry, a word that sounded like 'port' or was it 'pur?' So I asked, "Quel mot dites-vous – 'port'?" One of them called out "'Port', c'est comme 'harbour'." "Oh, je comprends," I answered, "port."

Then I added, "Est-ce-que le mot est masculin ou féminin?" One of them replied, "Masculin." When I enquired about their impression of 'le mer' along 'la côte d'Antrim,' I should have used the correct gender, 'la mer.' Confusing! "Non, non," one said, "c'est féminin." And we all laughed. I said, "Je pense que la langue française est sensuelle, mais aussi sexuelle parce que les mots, eux-mêmes, sont masculin ou féminin." Then we all laughed again. Later, I thought, "Well, of course, French is the language of Romance." Before the end of the week, both John and I began to find our French again, even coming up now and again with a joke.

One day John opened the door to discover Barry bent over his bike trying to 'break the bead' on one of the tires that had sprung a leak on the way back from Galway. While he hadn't been completely let down, nevertheless he had had to stop for air at garages every few miles. John, an experienced 'backyard mechanic,' joined him to see if he could help.

Before long, they had determined that the tire had picked up one of those long nails with a big head on it used to shoe horses. But between them they couldn't get the tire to separate from the rim. At home, John had a jack of a size that would have enabled him to break the bead, but the one that came with our rented car was incompatible.

Since we were heading to the other side of Omagh to visit Wilma that afternoon, we offered Barry a lift to the local garage mechanic. So in he climbed with his tire. Along the way he told us that his business frequently takes him to France and that, indeed, he and his wife have a "little shack," as he called it, in France for holidaying. "In fact," he said, "our daughter and French son-in-law have presented us with a little grandson. So, of course, that's a special reason for visiting over there." We let him off at the garage, and when we enquired how he would get back, he replied, "Don't worry about me. One of my friends is coming to get me."

The evening before our unusual neighbours were to depart, a knock came at our door. Barry stood there. "In an hour or so we're all going to share a slapdash pasta supper and we want you two Canadians to come. We hope you will." Of course, we wouldn't miss it!

As we entered, "Make way for the seniors!" and "Bonsoir, bonsoir, bienvenue" sounded in our ears. Then we were escorted to our places. The cooking was done in one cottage and we crowded into a larger cottage across the way to eat. Of course, the French had a wonderful assortment of wines, cheeses and baguettes, and the pasta and sauce were cooked by both the English and the French.

It warmed our hearts to see the camaraderie among this diverse group for conviviality abounded among them, no matter from what side of la Manche (the Channel) or westward across the Atlantic! In the morning we came out of our place to bid them "Au revoir, goodbye." There were handshakes and claps on shoulders all around. When they had gone off together in a gentle roar of engines, we stood still in the silence, punctuated by the sound of birdsong. Already, we could feel a rising sense of missing our unlikely neighbours who had touched our hearts with their peaceful initiative. Go well, I thought.

Gentle Little Visitors

I was sitting at the kitchen table by a window just at my elbow when a little face appeared. When I looked up a young boy of about nine or ten smiled at me and then in a second there was a quick knock at the door. As it turned out, he was Aidan or as it sounded to my ears, 'Awdan', delivered in two swift syllables, almost as one. He told me he was nine years old – the same age as our grandson John. Aidan had that lovely combination of glosssy black hair, fair skin and sharp blue eyes with tiny flecks of brown.

"Hello, Missus," he said, "I just walked down the path from the Centre and suddenly I saw these cottages. I live not too far from here, but I've never been inside one before. Where do yous come from?" he asked politely. "Canada," I answered. "Oh, a long way!" he noted. I introduced myself and John and then he said "Would yous mind letting me see what it's like inside?" (Several times I've noticed the plural use of 'you' so similar to the plural 'vous' in French, but sounding the 's'. I don't doubt the validity of its use in such an old country.)

And so we gave him the tour. He noted every feature ~ the many windows, the staircase leading to the landing with two windows looking out into the woods and downstairs, the big peat fireplace, with two colourful, upholstered chairs and the cosy cultyee in the corner. He communicated his keen interest, not with words, but by gazing about and now and again, with a little nod of his head. His own home would doubtless be a colourful, modern bungalow, likely a sunny yellow, with shining white or cobalt blue trim, like so many we saw throughout the countryside. But this little cottage in the woods, old-fashioned with its door of two halves must have seemed magical as in a fairy tale, complete with two white-haired folk, like grandparents.

"I must get back to the Centre," he said. "Today is Pentecost Sunday and my cousins and I and our families have just had a special meal in the restaurant after our First Communion in the parish church." He paused, "Would yous mind if I send my cousins to see this place?" Would we mind, I thought. We could hardly wait for them to arrive!

About ten minutes later, I glanced out the window toward the path. Four little girls, one about nine, two about six, and one not more than four, hurried toward our door. There were several quick, soft knocks and I welcomed them in. The newly confirmed girl, the nine-year-old, looked like a little bride or princess in a white lace-trimmed dress, decorated with a fresh rose and a white veil over her head ~ the traditional First Communion attire I remembered as a child in Quebec. The other little girls in every way implied they were her attendants, earnest and respectful in their demeanour.

The nine-year-old told us that she and her parents lived in the neighbourhood, as did her cousins. However, she and her family had recently returned from New York City, where they had lived for a time. She was the spokesperson for the group. "Where are you from?" (Her early education in the U.S. had erased the 's.') "Canada," I replied. "Oh, you would need an airplane for that."

"Do you go to the chapel?" she continued, a term I had noticed referring to the local Roman Catholic church. "At home, we call it 'church,'" I answered. "This is a special day for you, following your confirmation and First Communion." The child nodded, clasping her hands together for a moment while her little attendants nodded solemnly.

John and I looked at one another and smiled. "We remember our own Confirmation day," John said. He looked thoughtful and I guessed he was doing the math. "It was over sixty years ago in our church." Our visitors stared at us – to imagine the old ones as children was a bit of a stretch for them. "I remember wearing a white dress and veil that day and the boys in suits," I said. And again John and I looked at each other. "Do you know," he said to the children, "that the two of us were confirmed when we were twelve and thirteen and at the very same service all those years ago? And," he continued, "let's see if we remember what our bishop said as he placed his hands on our heads and prayed." Then together the two of us casting our minds back to our shared childhood, repeated, "Defend, O Lord, this thy servant with thy heavenly grace that she/he may continue thine for ever and daily increase in thy Holy Spirit more and more...." No sooner had he spoken the opening words than the little nine-year-old folded her hands for, of course they were the same words that she knew.

So I explained, "We belong to the Anglican Church of Canada; many of its traditions are similar to your own. You could say our church is catholic with a small 'c.' So I guess you could say our church is a cousin of yours." The children nodded. They already knew a lot about the significance of cousins.

Then their leader asked us a practical question. "How long is your service at home?" "About an hour and a half to two hours," I replied. "Ours is sometimes over three hours," she said, noting the difference, but making no comment. "Well," she said, "we have to get back to our families at the Centre." And they were off, all skipping, the newly confirmed girl leading the way and the little one, light as a feather, hurrying to catch up. Once, they turned and waved to us standing in the doorway.

In about twenty minutes, they were back! There they stood, each holding out to us tiny nosegays of freshly picked Michaelmas daisies. "Thank you, thank you," we repeated, our eyes close to brimming. Oh, children, I thought, God bless you and all the children of Ireland.

In a day or two we were on our way home and in my pack were tucked away, in dampened paper in a plastic bag, the tiny flowers. At home, tied to a little glass bird on a branch hanging in the dining-room window, the dried flowers still show their colours, visible in the sun shining through the window-pane.

Music Close to the Heart of Ireland

The poster on the wall at the Centre announced a concert on the coming Friday evening at 9:30 p.m., featuring three premier performers of Irish traditional music: Cathel Hayden, Martin O'Connor and Michael O'Domhnaill. As the Ulster Herald article said:

> From Tyrone, Galway and Donegal these musicians have been
> at the forefront of Irish music for the last number of years with
> various different bands, namely, Four Men and a Dog, De
> Dannan and Bothy Band. The three have toured extensively in
> Ireland, Europe and Japan bringing "their vibrant traditional
> music to enthusiastic followers."

"You're sure to enjoy yourselves," John Donaghy, the manager of the Centre, said. And so Tom, Sarah and I enjoyed an evening we will never forget; John, not quite rid of jet lag, missed it.

The opening duo was a young fiddler and guitarist, Donall Donnelly from nearby BallyGalley, and Deirdre Murray from Randalstown. Both are accomplished musicians, appearing throughout Ireland in concert. Donall, himself, has toured widely in Europe, South Africa and North America. Over the years of visiting the whole of Ireland, we have witnessed the extensive revival of Irish traditional music, starting with the teaching of children and youth who as they grow into adulthood become accomplished musicians like Donall and Deirdre. It goes without saying that in Ireland, music knows no boundaries.

Sitting in the front row of the theatre, we were just a few feet from the players. Such melding of the music with the very expressiveness of the young players, their bodies swaying, their feet tapping to the tunes, their hands dancing as fingers met strings! The two left the stage to thunderous applause, expressing the pride of those gathered who could claim them as their own.

John Donaghy left the theatre for a few minutes and then returned to say that the three stars were just arriving. He held up his hand to make an announcement. "The musicians have stipulated that no smoking is allowed during the performance." And I thought, "This, indeed, is a special performance; after all, it is a theatre, not a pub." He opened the door and three men entered, not young, perhaps from mid-forties to mid-fifties. The crowd was quiet as the musicians took their seats on the same level as the first row, where Tom, Sarah and I sat.

On the left sat the fiddler, Cathel Hayden, almost Spanish looking, with black curls, a mustache and dark eyes full of seriousness. In the middle, playing the button accordion, was Martin O'Connor, his hair grey and longish, his blue eyes barely concealing a smile. The guitarist, Michael O'Domhnaill, had a depth to his hazel eyes that made me think, This fellow has the look of a story teller about him. Indeed, not only did he play, but sang and told stories. John welcomed them and then turned to Martin O'Connor who was the spokesperson for the group.

No sooner had he named the tunes coming up than they were away in a flash and so were we all, riding on the heartfelt traditional music. My feet could not keep still ~ this was the rhythm of the first music I ever knew, so familiar to my Irish-Quebec people. Indeed, the tunes carried across the ocean nearly two hundred years ago appear to have been claimed and renamed to affirm them as their own. For they were familiar, 'driving' reels, like 'Reel Montreal' and 'Reel St. Jean' and the beautiful, slow tempo of 'Valse Parisienne'.

All the time, the tunes were accompanied by the dancing feet of Michael O'Conner, the accordion player, and the swaying upper-bodies of the fiddler and guitarist. Only occasionally would Michael look up at the audience and smile at our feet, keeping time to the music while the other two remained engrossed in the tunes.

Then, in and out of the music that lifted my heart, I remembered my grandmother, who loved this music. In spite of a stroke in her early sixties, she would come with the rest of us to the dances, and not just to sit still on the bench. For keeping time with her one good foot, her cane laid aside, she rode on the music that had crossed the sea from Ireland to Quebec before she was born.

The fiddler had a serious face like a classical violinist, and his feet were more restrained than the others. But, oh, the bow in his hand was a flash as it danced over the strings, the tune filling the air and wafting over us. The guitarist had long-fingered hands that drew the music out, almost lovingly, his large eyes seeming to reflect the various moods of the music. He was a singer with a voice of rich tones, capable of expressing a myriad of emotions: pathos, love and humour.

At one point he sang 'Ye Take the High Road and I'll Take the Low Road', but first introduced the song with a touch of history: "Her lover was in jail, being on the wrong side of the powers that be." Essentially, the singer told us her lover was telling the woman, "Get the hell out while you can, for I'm not going to make it out of here alive." Then the song followed ~ it seemed old and it seemed new, even contemporary, and brought tears to my eyes as the troubadour sang his story.

A RETURN TO THE CITY OF LONDONDERRY

Looking Back

In the 1980s, John and I had visited for the first time the city of Londonderry in the Ulster county by the same name, referred to by some as 'Derry'. It truly is a northern city with the magnificent Foyle River and its wide estuary on the last lap of its journey to the sea and the Antrim coast. Straight out from that coast, ranging from rugged embankments battered by waves higher than a tall building to sheltered beaches, landfall would be Iceland.

On that particular visit, the 'Troubles' of Northern Ireland had been underway for over a decade with signs of boarded-up buildings, broken windows, cracked pavement, and pockmarked walls marred by explosives and fire. And everywhere were young British soldiers in tanks and helicopters. On our way into the city, we had been stopped just once by the police and asked for our driver's licenses and passports, and then, gratefully, waved on ahead.

As we had entered the city from a southeasterly direction, we caught sight of St. Columb's, the Church of Ireland cathedral, standing on a promontory overlooking the slope of the city running down to the Foyle. We drove up the hill, taking note of the surrounding ancient wall of Londonderry. Built in the early 1640s, it is one of the oldest in Ireland. We wondered how many times in its history had it been under assault and yet it still stands.

The cathedral doors were open, but the stained-glass windows were boarded up, perhaps even removed. As we entered, the verger had come forward to meet us. As it turned out, he was an amateur historian and genealogist. When I told him that my father's ancestors by the name of Canning had likely come from County Londonderry and that I had already noticed a good number of Cannings listed in the phone book, he nodded his head. "But there is evidence that the name has a Viking connection," he said. "Many family names that end in 'ing' have a such a connection."

Later, we asked him where in the city he could recommend a place for us to eat. He directed us to a newly built small shopping mall with a good restaurant where, he added, "the folk will look after you." That was so, for we were accepted in such a welcoming way with nods and smiles, as if we were frequent visitors. Of course, we were well aware that visitors like us were as rare as hen's teeth in such a setting of destruction. When we told them we were from Canada, someone asked if we had any connection with the north. "Through my ancestors who left these parts in the 1820s for Quebec. I have wanted to come here for a long time," I replied.

Later in the day, before leaving the city to drive back down to Wilma's bed and breakfast, we had stopped at a small cafe for afternoon tea and scones. A number of townspeople were there for the same reason, including young women with babies in prams and older folk. As John and I were getting settled and began to speak together quietly, several people looked our way. "How are you?" someone asked, not "Where are you from?" The greeting was both cordial and casual, not very different from how they greeted their neighbours. We drank our tea and ate our scones along with the others while once more smiles and nods were sent our way.

Suddenly a loud siren sounded in the street and all grew quiet, including the babies. We waited along with them, relaxing finally when the others picked up the threads of their conversation. Silence followed the siren and in a few minutes some got up to leave and so did we. Then someone asked, "Where are you from?" John replied, "Canada," more nods followed. "Have you people here?" another asked. "No," I said, "but I'm descended from those who left the north a hundred years before I was born," adding, "in many ways it feels like home." And I thought, For it is the people that make it so.

It had been my first visit to Londonderry;, and little did I know then that our visit in the spring of 2004 would reveal by sheer coincidence two Canning cousins in Northern Ireland. While they live in more easterly parts of the north, their family origins lie both in County Londonderry (Derry) and the adjacent Donegal County, the most northerly part of the Republic of Ireland.

In the intervening years between the 1980s and 2000, we had stayed away from Derry City, traveling only along the Antrim Coast in rural areas and in nearby Donegal. The reason? Because of the resurgence of the Troubles. But by 2004, we had already discovered some glad news through communication from Irish friends over there, through the media and from our own reading. The peace initiative had been gaining ground over the last few years, after a very discouraging stall in 2000. Indeed, Canada's own General John de Chastelain, who is from Alberta and is an experienced peacekeeper, has played a key role in such an initiative.

Travel writers in the 2003-2004 books, particularly *The Lonely Planet*, had been reconnoitering the situation on the ground in Northern Ireland. The result? They were lavish in their praise of the emerging of this 'unspoiled country', its varied beauty, the warmth and creativity of its people and the presence of its longed-for peace and quiet. Writers of such books were even projecting the view that in a couple of years Northern Ireland would be a destination of choice by many people, even going so far as to say, "don't wait too long to go."

John and I took satisfaction in what our visits over twenty-five years had taught us about the beauty of Northern Ireland, but especially in the steady welcome and warm hospitality we received from its people in spite of the harsh reality of the Troubles. Recently, I read a book by Dervla Murphy from the Republic of Ireland written about her very first visit in the mid-1970s to the North. Already an intrepid cyclist in many countries of Europe and Asia, she began to question her long-standing reluctance to cross the northern border. It was time, she decided, to take her courage in her hands and enter that 'Place Apart'.

Traveling north, she eventually entered the city of Derry and before long, through conversations with folk of different ages and in people's homes, where hospitality was offered and in pubs, she was struck by their willingness to speak with her in spite of her being from the Republic. Soon she sought out opportunities to speak with the youth and was greatly impressed by their keen insights into the Troubles and its impact upon their lives. Two young men, home from their university studies in Belfast, spoke to Dervla Murphy about the challenge to adjust to the wider community of young people that the university presented, so different from the individual church-affiliated schools of their earlier education. Yet, the young men conveyed that engaging in the challenge might lead to peace. This chapter she called 'Derry is Different', and I agree.

Derry Transformed

In our 2004 visit, Tom and Sarah wanted to visit Derry. So one bright morning, we set out to spend the day there. The contrast for John and me was astonishing. The harvest of the Peace Initiative, which had been unfolding during the previous four years, was as shining as the day. The cathedral's stained-glass windows glowed in the sunlight. Lively groups of children in school uniforms passed by, full of chat and laughter. Shoppers, laden with fresh produce from the supermarkets, headed toward their cars.

People gathered in cafes painted in bright colours outside and in ~ bright orange, cobalt blue trimmed in shining white; others paused to survey the mouthwatering displays in bakery windows before entering. Shoppers passed steadily through the doors of a department store, resplendent with vaulted glass ceilings revealing the sky. There were wide aisles for strolling and comfortably appointed upholstered chairs for weary shoppers to rest, as in some stores here at home.

We had our lunch in an already crowded pub on a corner. It had tables and chairs on two levels, the upper one overlooking the lower one. Young people abounded, enjoying their noon break marked by lively chat and bursts of laughter. We found a table for four upstairs and soon a young woman came to take our orders. Both the north and the south of Ireland have excellent training centres in the culinary arts; the food was delicious.

When it came time to pay the bill, John asked our server a question he frequently asks at home. "Is it the practice in this place to share the gratuities among the staff? Because at home in Canada it isn't always done that way and I think that's not fair to the people who serve." New at her job, she replied, "Oh, I would think so, but just wait a moment and I'll go ask."

In a few minutes the manager came out with the server. Both of them were smiling. "Here comes an ambiguous Irish trick," I thought. And indeed it was so. He walked up to John and said "Are you the fellow from Canada who's trying to corrupt my staff?" What followed was time out for a few minutes of friendly chat among the six of us, and it soon became apparent that the practice followed was certainly not the way in the 'New World'.

After our lunch, we entered a tourist information centre not far from the Foyle River. It was a bright, spacious building with shelves displaying glossy, colourful brochures, describing the visitor attractions of the city. There were, for example, "the historic walls of Derry, built early in the 17th century, making it the only remaining completely walled city in Ireland, and one of the finest examples in Europe of Walled Cities;" St. Columb's Cathedral, built in 1633; Foyle Cruises; The Workhouse Museum advertising the Atlantic Memorial, "an exhibition of the effects on the city and the role the city played during the Battle of the Atlantic;" and finally, "Famine," an exhibition on the Great Hunger in Ireland.

On the back of one of the brochures was a picture of a young man, stretched out with hands behind his head, dozing in a rowboat with oars stowed, a straw hat pulled down over his eyes, just drifting on the Foyle beyond the charming Foyle side area. The area, newly restored, is a delight for strolling, shopping and enjoying gathering places such as pubs, restaurants and green places that invite the passersby to take their ease on the grass or the handy benches, while the magnificent Foyle is just there for the looking.

Sarah and Tom were delighted with the city, while John and I, equally delighted, felt deeply moved by the vibrant city before our eyes in contrast with the memory of our first visit during the Troubles twenty-six years earlier. After returning home, I brought out the beautiful brochures I had packed away. I found myself staring at the picture of the totally relaxed young man drifting on the Foyle in his row-boat as he obviously enjoyed the peace of the slowly moving river. Oh, youth of Ireland, I thought, you have waited long for this peace initiative, many of you growing up, knowing the Troubles seemed never to go away. Go well.

Surprised by Coincidence

During our 1979 visit to Omagh, County Tyrone in Northern Ireland, I had met Jim Canning whose striking resemblance to my father's people nearly bowled John and me over, as well as our son Jack, who accompanied us. Jim, himself, looked at Jack and pronounced, "He's a Canning." It was obvious to us parents as we looked at their profiles. That day Jim told us that while he had lived in Tyrone many years, most Cannings came from County Derry. In a subsequent visit to Ireland, we were sad to hear that Jim Canning had died. As the Troubles continued during subsequent visits, we didn't linger long in that county.

However, this past spring, after perusing the bountiful array of brochures, I approached a man behind the desk. "My family name is Canning. My Canning ancestors emigrated to Quebec in 1827. Unfortunately, archival material of that period was burned in Dublin about 1921." He nodded. "Do you know any Cannings in this area?" "I don't personally but certainly it's a name you hear of in these parts," he replied. "But just wait a minute while I get the telephone book." I smiled.

In a matter of minutes, he had run off a copy of a page and a half of all the Cannings in Northern Ireland, many of them in this county. He underlined each name with a yellow marker. I thanked him heartily, folded the paper and tucked it away in my purse. I could feel my heart lift.

A few days later, while exploring the Antrim coast toward the east, Tom pulled into a lay-by, reached by a series of turnings in the road, to admire the view. This allowed us to look back from where we had come, across a valley and toward the sea. A moment later another car pulled up beside us. Tom had just stepped out of the car when the driver 'next door' did the same. Soon they were in conversation. They were talking about the view but, suddenly, the man asked Tom if we had any ancestral connection with the north. Then I heard Tom refer to our Canning ancestors.

In a moment, his wife was out of the car, leaning through the car window to speak to me. "I know Mr. Thomas Canning who lives in Armagh not far from where we live. He was my history teacher in high school and a very good one. He's retired now," she continued, "It's a pity I don't remember his phone number, but I know where his house is. What we need is a phone book," she declared. I nodded.

Suddenly a light went on in my head. "Wait a minute," I nearly shouted. "But I do have a page of it. Last week the tourist office man in Derry ran off a copy that includes all the Cannings in Northern Ireland. What have I been thinking of? It's right here in my purse!" Margaret Brownlee, as was her name, was nearly as excited as I was. "Let's have a look!" Together we quickly scanned the page. And there I read, Thomas Canning, Master of Education, complete with phone number and address. Beside me, Margaret, delighting to confirm the information, said, "Oh, you must get in touch with him." Before we parted with the Brownlees, they gave us their phone number. "You must call to let us know how your meeting went." Unfortunately, we were unable to meet them again as they were leaving very soon on a holiday.

Cliffs at the sea edge

John, Tom and Laurel on the Antrim Coast after meeting the Browlees

Close to a Miracle

The following few days were busy ones, driving Sarah to the Belfast City airport when her week with us was up and later, to do the same for Tom when his ten days had come to an end. One evening early in the week, following their departure, I picked up the phone and dialed Tom Canning's number. A woman with a pleasing voice in a soft Northern Ireland accent answered. In a rush of words I declared, "My name is Mona Laurel Canning Buck from Canada. My Canning ancestors immigrated to Quebec in 1827. A few days ago I met a former student of Thomas Canning, Margaret Brownlee is her name." Before I could rattle on anymore, the woman said, "I'm Elizabeth Canning, Tom's wife, and I can tell you he will want to talk with you."

For a few moments, time stood still for me. Then he picked up the receiver and I heard, "Where are you?" "In County Tyrone," (bordering County Armagh, to the west), I replied. "We're located half way between Omagh and Cookstown." "That's not far from us," Tom said. "You must come to visit." Then, "Just a moment." A pause followed then I heard, "Elizabeth, are you ready to have two visitors from Canada?" "Yes," she replied, "How about Sunday for lunch?" And so it was arranged.

I pause here to explain that in all likelihood, my Canning ancestors sailed in 1827 from Ireland to Quebec on the ship, the *George Canning*. It was named for George Canning, Prime Minister of Great Britain from April 10th, 1827 until his untimely death in August of that year. Formerly, he had been Minister of Foreign Affairs in William Pitt's government and some years later, his son, Charles, became the first Viceroy of India.

Incidentally, my mother's ancestors by the name of Little likely sailed on the same ship, settling on land not far from my Canning ancestors. I believe my mother's ancestors were farmers from the beginning because, having settled in the Appalachian hills of Megantic County near Quebec City, generations later they continued to farm until some years after World War II.

While it is true that several of my Grandfather Little's siblings had migrated to Vermont and the Carolinas, as many stayed on in Megantic County. I believe the Littles were farmers by nature; it was in the blood. It is interesting that Littles and Marshalls (Marshall being my maternal grandmother's name) we have come to know in Northern Ireland still farm and bear a resemblance to those in Quebec by the same names.

The Cannings, on the other hand, had become scarce on the ground even when I was a child, a number of them becoming urbanized in Montreal, New Britain and Hartford, Connecticut, New York and Albany. The Cannings I knew had a talent to work with wood. My father's brother, Lambert, was a good carpenter; when I was a child on the farm, he made me a little sleigh, painted blue, which I used not only for sliding, but for pulling through the deep snow in the barnyard to 'make roads'.

My father's brother, Mark, worked for many years in Montreal's highly respected Fraser Brothers, where fine furniture from the estates of influential Montrealers was put up for auction. His uncle, Stuart Robinson, as manager of the business, encouraged Mark to develop the aesthetic sense his uncle observed in him. I recall that my great-uncle Stuart himself shared this sense; in particular, I remember a collection of Chinese pottery in his Montreal apartment. In fact, for a time, he engaged himself in study of the Chinese language.

My father, during the Depression of the 1930s, eased the boredom of long hours of work in a flour mill in Montreal harbour by working with wood at night in the coal shed behind our flat in Verdun. Wood from my grandfather Little's sugar bush was fashioned into a bookcase of maple trimmed with cherry, complete with glass doors, framed in wood, and decorated with small brass handles. Today it resides in our dining room. I write at a desk he made over sixty years ago. It has three shelves down one side and a drawer with a carved handle, all of the same kinds of wood as the bookcase. He even made my sister and me a dollhouse, complete with rooms tastefully furnished. I recollect that, as childhood disappeared in time, the dollhouse was passed on to much younger cousins. My father would have been pleased....

But that particular Sunday morning in 2004 dawned and as I rose, I could feel the excitement building in me. I wondered, What if I had left the copy of the listing of Cannings back in our little Irish cottage? What if our son, Tom, hadn't got out of the car to speak to the Brownlees, telling them of my family name, Canning? What if Margaret Brownlee hadn't been there to tell me about Thomas Canning, her former teacher?

It was a sunny spring morning as we began our drive east to Armagh City, passing through soft green valleys and up and over hills, clad in burgeoning woods. We swept past a sign to the right leading to Six Mile Town. Soon we reached a steep hill leading down to the town of Ballygawley, close to the M1 superhighway and heading east to the County of Armagh.

That county is noted for its apple orchards, particularly for a variety called Bramley, which are ideally suited for the baking of pies, cakes, turnovers, and sauce. As we drove toward the city of the same name, orchards began to appear more and more, glowing with a bounty of pink blossoms against a constant backdrop of soft green fields and wooded hills. Soon, the spires of the two cathedrals built on hills and named for Saint Patrick came into view.

Years before we had visited both cathedrals, more as tourists, but in 2004 we were on a mission to meet Cannings. However, we had a problem. What road to take to arrive at the Cannings' home a few miles beyond the centre of the city? Its layout, like many old cities, seemed a maze with spokes reaching out in different directions. We stopped outside the Church of Ireland cathedral grounds to seek information.

A couple strolling nearby were the very ones to help. They had been enjoying a few days' holiday in the city and were about to return home. When they heard of the Cannings' address they said, "That's the direction we're going in. Just follow us and we'll show you the way." And so we did, our two 'forerunners' waving at us, pointing out the turn toward the Cannings' road.

Face to Face

Soon we spotted the house on our left, set within the embrace of a curving garden at the back and a field with a cluster of beehives across the road. My experience has often told me, Every Irish person loves a field, and those who have lost one never forget it. Just as we stepped out of the car, the door of the house opened. Taking off my sunhat, I looked up to see a tall man of retirement age standing there. He was staring at me in amazement, his hand up to his mouth. "Why you look just like Sarah Canning. I can't believe it! She was my aunt." I, myself, was struck by his appearance, tall like my uncle Mark, with dark hair and blue eyes set in a characteristic sharp, intent look I had often observed in my people.

Tom Canning welcomed us in. Fetching Elizabeth, he presented John and me almost with formality, "This is Mona Laurel Canning Buck from Canada and her husband, John." Then, "Now, who do you think Laurel looks like?" "Oh," she replied with a smile, "like a Canning." For a moment I felt tears stinging my eyes, as I stood there in their sunny living room looking out upon their vibrant garden.

I thought of my father's family overshadowed by so much loss ~ there was the tragic loss of their father and the foreclosure of the homestead that had been in the family over a hundred years. I thought of the deaths of my grandparents' three infant children between 1904 and 1907 and then Mona, in 1924, of bone cancer at the age of twelve. How often the descendants of such immigrants were shattered by such losses in that period of our history! No wonder the stories my father might have told me lay buried for so long. For a moment or two, I seemed lost in thoughts of the past. But John stood beside me and Tom and Elizabeth Canning were looking at me with smiles.

"Your name, Laurel, is an unusual name here in Ireland," Elizabeth remarked. I nodded. "I was baptized Mona Laurel, Mona having an Irish connection, but I've always been called by my second name. My parents from Quebec lived in New Britain, Con-

65

necticut for five years where I was born in 1927. I have noticed that 'Laurel' appears more frequently in the U.S. Their climate must be more conducive to laurel bushes than in Canada." She smiled.

Soon we were settled comfortably in their living room. Tom looked at John and me. "We want to hear about your coming to Ireland this spring and about where you live in Canada. But I've phoned my cousin Bill, who, unlike me, is a good amateur genealogist. He lives in the town of Antrim and will be arriving shortly to meet you and then we'll have lunch together."

Before long we could hear a car pulling up at the front door. Tom rose from his chair and went to the door. I could hear Tom greeting his cousin. Several seconds passed and suddenly Bill looked around the corner of the room at me. There was a pause. "I would say you look like Aunt Sarah!" Tom laughed, "I never mentioned to Bill who you look like. I just told him to take a peek." And we all laughed. Unfortunately, I discovered that she had died years ago, their beloved aunt whom I would never meet. Both cousins are trying to track down a picture of her. It seems true that in periods of unrest and upheaval in a country, taking frequent family photos is not a priority.

Bill had the same blue eyes as Tom, but a shorter figure, sturdy and muscular, like my father. He came with pages of genealogical material, and as I perused them, I noted that their Cannings were related to Robinsons. I gasped, "I see that your forebears include Cannings and Robinsons. I must tell you that in Quebec that is also the case. My paternal grandparents were Henry Francis Canning and Sarah Robinson. Perhaps that is behind the striking resemblance you see between me and Sarah Canning."

There was a moment of quiet in the room. It was Elizabeth who spoke. "As you say, your ancestors left here in 1827, one hundred and seventy-some years ago. But over here that's not considered a very long time ago." Then Tom, looking across the room at his cousin, said, "Perhaps you have turned up some data that connects George Canning with our Cannings. He was one of Pitt's ministers and later became Prime Minister of Britain in 1827. How serious are you, Bill, about that idea?" Bill acknowledged that he thought it was not too far-fetched an idea.

I could scarcely wait to tell them what I had to say about it. I looked at John who was smiling at me. I began. "Years ago when I was a child in Verdun (Montreal) during the Great Depression, Bob Canning, a cousin of my father and his wife from New York landed at our door. His old car had barely made it. So it became an extended visit while Bob worked on the car until finally it was once more ready for the road." I paused, remembering how I had felt as a child.

"Relations between my father and his cousin seemed somewhat strained and I wondered about that. Even then I knew that money was in short supply. But there was something else.

"One day cousin Bob began his story telling, a practice so familiar to me in our Irish-Canadian farm community (for although then a New Yorker, he had come from that same Megantic farm community as the rest of us)." Then I went on to say that Bob began to tell about how the Cannings who came to Quebec were connected with a prominent Canning who had held an important post in the British government. I recall asking my father about Bob's story. He would shake his head, muttering, "Those Canning cousins like to brag about that." It was never spoken of again. "So," I concluded, "that story obviously crossed the Atlantic nearly two hundred years ago."

Again there was quiet in the room. And then Elizabeth announced that lunch was ready. Before Bill Canning had to leave, he presented John and me with a copy of his book about the contribution made by the young men from the farms of Ulster and Donegal during World War I. He, now in his sixties, had served in the military as a young man in various international peace initiatives. In the last number of years he has worked as an executive of the Parkinson's Disease Foundation, traveling widely to raise awareness of the need for continuing research into possible treatments for this debilitating disease. Interestingly, among some I have known in my old community, there have been a significant number of cases of Parkinson's disease.

After John and I had returned home to Calgary, I opened his book. My eyes were caught by Bill's picture as a young man in full uniform on the back cover. His profile was part way turned toward the camera. What I saw sent me scrambling to put my father's picture as a young man alongside Bill's. The profiles were almost identical! Then glancing through the book, I came across a picture of Samuel Canning in full face to the camera. He had been a great uncle of Bill Canning, but died as a young man as a result of his service in World War I.

I stared at the picture. The resemblance to my Cannings was striking, even down to the set of the ears! One ear was close to the head, while the other was cupped away from the head. I had only to check in the mirror to see the set of my odd ear, in my case the right. I am not the only one with such a set, for in an old photo of my grandfather, Henry Francis Canning, with my grandmother, Sarah Robinson, and three of their children, my grandfather's prominent left ear stands out.

Of course, I wrote to Bill to tell him of the likenesses I had noted and sent him the picture of my father and of my paternal grandparents. I could not resist commending him for the tone of his book's introduction. For not only is there tenderness expressed in the story of his great-uncle Samuel's sad demise at the age of nineteen, but also in Bill's description of the farmhouse where he grew up in northern Donegal, just across the border from County Derry.

In a letter enclosed among several pages of Canning genealogy, he said that in spite of the loss of archival material covering the period of emigration to Quebec in the 1820s, given the resemblances noted in the pictures and the Canning/Robinson family connections in Ireland and Quebec, the likelihood of our being related is strong. In retrospect, I see that behind the meeting between the Canning cousins and me, stand Elizabeth Canning and my John, both witnesses to the sincerity of the emotions reflected in our Canning faces and voices. That is a comfort in itself, not to be forgotten.

That day after Bill Canning had left, Tom invited us to go for a drive to see the Bramley variety of apple orchards. We were not prepared for the sight of acres and acres stretching for miles on both sides of the route Tom took. Here, without a doubt, was the very heart of the Armagh orchards. It was a wonderland of spreading apple trees as far as the eye could see. The branches were lavishly adorned with shining pink blossoms, their fragrance carried on the spring air. Spring in that part of Armagh could not help but cause the heart to lift up, as the shimmering green of the fields and hills embraced the glory of the Armagh orchards.

On the way back, Tom drove by a beautiful old stone church with stained-glass windows and a stately cemetery that spoke of lives lived for generations from that area. Tom slowed the car for a few minutes. "Many of my people are buried there," he said. "It has been the church where generations of my family have worshipped. But it's closed now." John and I wanted to know why. "I'll tell you, but first I want to show you something," he replied. Not far away he slowed the car again and pointed to a new church, its design geometric in a sharp, angular way.

Tom told us that the closing of old churches is to be followed by more new churches being built. "But what will become of the old ones?" we wondered. "I think," Tom replied sadly, "they will remain standing, but we know of no plan to preserve what is inside them. I predict that what will happen is they will be vandalized." And we could see the sorrow and sense of loss on his face.

Returning home to Elizabeth, the four of us sat down to the tasty afternoon tea she had prepared for us. We bade *au revoir* to one another, rather wistfully, I felt. Indeed, a connection had been made that was vital in itself. For, without being spoken of, the presence of those Cannings who, in time past, had lived and died on both sides of the Atlantic, seemed close at hand.

The Importance of Cousins

A couple of days after our visit to Armagh, the phone rang in our little Irish cottage. It was Bill Canning. "My sister, Frances, has been in conversation with James and Maude Robinson in Donegal. James is related to the Cannings. Both are in their eighties. They would like a visit with you and here is their phone number. They live on a farm in Burt, just over the border from County Derry." I was delighted to hear this and soon John had the map out to check the location.

Maude answered. She immediately got to the point because after all, our meeting had been arranged within the extended family. "Can you come tomorrow? I have a doctor's appointment today. Come in the morning and later we'll have some lunch. I won't put James on the phone because he's hard of hearing and when you come you'll have to speak up," she said with a smile in her voice. "Now, here are the directions how to get to us."

We left our little cottage early in the morning, driving northwest to Strabane where we would cross the Foyle River into Donegal. Between John and me, on the seat, were Maude's directions.

As we approached the town, we were astonished to see a magnificent collection of larger than life, stylized human figures, fashioned out of steel and mounted on a rise. They depicted a band of Celtic musicians in full flight, so to speak, totally caught up in their tunes. The effect was breathtaking and then I felt the quick tears coming. For Strabane had known much distress during the Troubles. The artist, it seemed to me, had created both a piece of art and a message of peace.

Maude's directions carried us northward over rising hills; on our left, the tidal river, the Swilly, ran swiftly to the sea. Maude had suggested that we use the service station, Nat Oil, as a landmark of where to turn up into the hills leading to Burt. When we stopped at the station, a man was just coming out. He quickly confirmed that we were on the right track. "Everyone knows James and Maude. Keep going on the road as it climbs. Their farm is on

70

the right, almost at the end before the road starts to come down to the highway." Maude had said, "When you reach our place, you'll see 'Toulett' on the gate." At first I had thought that she meant 'To Let', but the man told us that is, indeed, the name of the farm.

As we drove higher and higher through the hills, we saw the height of land directly ahead, and on the right there was the little gate announcing, Toulett. As we got out of the car, two dogs in the yard came to greet us, with wagging tails and boisterous barking. The door opened and James called to the dogs to be quiet. Maude appeared by his side, and we were welcomed into the Robinsons' comfortable kitchen.

As I had found with the Cannings, the voices of Maude and James, softly accented, had the same inflections as my people in Megantic County, Quebec. In fact, it is only as I write these lines now, almost a year later that I realize how true it is. Indeed, so familiar was their speech that I simply found my place in it, hardly realizing how amazing this was, given the intervening generations.

Maude, sharp of eye, keen of hearing and quick in her moving about her kitchen, was the talkative one. James had just come from feeding the hens and was content to rest in his chair. I sensed that his health was not robust. As he said, "I'm retired and don't keep animals as I used to. We used to own seven farms but not anymore." Did I detect a wistful note in his voice? He spoke quietly (like Earl Robinson, a cousin of my father's, who farmed in my old Megantic County), then he added, "Cannings and Robinsons are related and around here is where most of us lived in days gone by."

Then Maude spoke up. "Over the last few years some Robinsons and Cannings from the U.S. and Canada have come looking for information about their ancestors." James smiled, "When the first one came, I hesitated to let him in: I guess I thought he might have been a tax collector." This little joke, very familiar to me, proved that while his health might not be robust, his sense of humour was lively.

"Years ago," Maude began to reminisce, "a man came to our door from Cumbria in England's Lake District. His name was David Moore Robinson. Stories of the origin of his family were largely unknown to him. However, he had discovered a gravestone in the countryside where he was born bearing the name of someone with the same family names as his, someone born in Burt, Donegal. He was in luck for we were able to show the very place his Robinson forebears had lived. We have since claimed one another as members of the Robinson family and he frequently visits us."

As we drank our tea and enjoyed Maude's cookies, I listened to the conversation of the other three and gazed at James Robinson. His facial features were familiar. He was taller than my Robinson cousins from Quebec, but not as dark as some. But when I closed my eyes, listening to his voice, I found his manner of expressing himself so like those I had long known. There in that kitchen, I felt at rest.

It was Maude who told us that neither of their two sons farmed ~ so like my Robinson and Canning relatives in Quebec. One of Maude and James's sons works in the recording industry, often going on tour with professional singers, such as Mary Black. The other son works in the production of software for computer companies.

Soon our hosts learned that John is an ordained Anglican minister, an honorary assistant at Christ Church in Calgary. It began when Maude described a Church of Ireland minister and his wife and family who, years ago, had served in that area. "We became real friends, although we are Presbyterians. I suppose they felt they could relax with us and would drop by for tea." Apparently he had served in a far-flung mission field where his health had been affected. As to the Robinsons' own minister, she noted that he has several churches to look after and "doesn't have time for himself, let alone much visiting."

There was a turn in our conversation, and as I've seen in our travels many times, some folk we have met will begin to speak with John as if he were their pastor. It's a very precious thing to witness, and indeed, such occasions have shaped our awareness that travel can be a kind of pilgrimage, both for us and those we have met on the way. A kind of community develops because of what is exchanged between us.

At some point, John asked James and Maude if it would not be out of place for him to take a prayer for the two of them and their home. They smiled and nodded. There was a moment of quiet, and then John prayed for our hosts, for Toulett, giving thanks for their hospitality to us two Canadians. Afterwards, they thanked John. "It was like having a visit from our old friend."

Maude had encouraged me to phone David Moore Robinson right away. I did and soon found myself talking with another enthusiastic story teller. His voice sounded like a young man and yet, he was not. I learned later that he is seventy. Perhaps enthusiasm about the sudden discovery of potential kin creates a timbre in one's voice that is quite distinct.

After John and I had returned home last spring, I was speaking with a friend at church. She is a native of northern Donegal but has lived many years in Canada. "Where did you go on your trip to Northern Ireland?" Mary asked me one Sunday. I gave her a brief description and then told her about meeting, quite by chance, two people by the name of Canning. "They are related to Robinsons in Donegal and before John and I came home we had a visit with them," I told her. "Where in Donegal?" she asked. "Not far from the city of Derry," I answered. "What place?" "In Burt," I replied. Mary's eyes became very bright. "And what is the name of their place?" I said, "It's an unusual name, Toulett." Mary put her hand over her mouth. "Laurel, I know them. I'm from Burt and I've known them all my life."

In fact, Mary's family is associated with Robinsons and Cannings, either as neighbours or relatives or both. But one thing I know: Mary's family name being Porter and the association with Robinsons and Cannings may well reflect the community that my forebears left in 1827. For Porter, too, is a family name in Megantic County, Quebec. One day I said to Mary, "I grew up with a Porter: her name was Rita and she had red hair." Mary looked at me closely, "My sister has red hair!"

One more story of Cannings came to light just before Christmas, 2004. My son Martin sent me a copy of an internet posting he had seen ~ a woman looking for other Cannings whose ancestors emigrated from Ireland to Inverness, Megantic County, in 1827. I looked at the data she had provided and I became very excited. For when I consulted the data I have of my Canning ancestors, there was her grandfather's name and he was my own grandfather's brother! When we spoke on the phone, I was surprised to hear her accent. She was born in New Jersey, as were her parents, and her accent was rich in those distinctive New Jersey tones.

She grew up hearing no ancestral stories about Ireland, nor Megantic County, Quebec. It pained her, therefore, that she had nothing to tell her own children. At first I assumed that since our grandfathers had been brothers, she must be a senior like me. Not so, for she is the same age as our eldest son, Martin, fifty-three. The reason? Neither her grandfather nor her father were young when they married, whereas my grandfather and father were.

We spoke for nearly forty-five minutes that first time and later I sent her a copy of my first book, *Stream of Memory: Reflections of Megantic County, Quebec*. Shortly after it arrived at her home, she phoned me. "Laurel," she said in an excited tone, "your book has just arrived and when I opened the package, it was the back cover with your picture that met my eyes. I could hardly believe it! I could have been looking in the mirror. I showed it to my daughter and she has just confirmed that." I, myself, was amazed for those were the same words I had heard from Tom and Bill Canning last spring in Armagh, "You look almost identical to Sarah Canning."

Yesterday, I phoned Tom Canning in Armagh to tell him about a new-found American cousin. Of course, he was interested. I asked if he had any success in finding the picture of Sarah Canning, his aunt who died years ago. "Not yet, but if one exists after all these years, you can be sure I'll send you a copy. If not," Tom added, "all you have to do is look in the mirror!"

In retrospect, I can see how surprising it is that my visits to Ireland since 1979, armed with no genealogical data except for a few fragments of story telling, told by the old ones in Megantic County, should have been anything more than a frustrating wild-goose chase. But the references to places somehow had stuck in my mind since childhood; that coupled with my deeply felt desire to go there, to see the country as a whole and then to enter the north, expecting to see strong resemblance between my people and those with the same family names.

To have not been disappointed in my quest, but so enriched by those I've met over the years by the same family names is a heartfelt blessing. For just as the Irish Marshalls and Littles, whom we first met twenty-five years ago, attest to the striking resemblance among us, now the Canning/Robinsons assure me "just look in the mirror." The set of the eyes, the turn of an ear and the manner of speaking are, themselves, imprints not to be ignored.

STORIES IN POEMS, PROSE & LETTERS

Negative to Positive

I open my Christmas card
from Dorothy, friend of my farm days,
inside I find a negative...
"This has to be you and
your parents, I think."
I hold it up to the light.
Against the dark
of the background, three
figures etched, visitors at the annual
picnic in the farm community
that once was ours.
Why do I hold my breath
for a moment?
What cloud emanates from
the dark background?
Why is my father there? He,
indentured like a slave to
a seven-day work week,
knew life was no picnic
in the "Great" Depression!

Later, the negative, developed,
lies in my palm
a raw moment of
conflict exposed.
The three of us stand,
my parents facing the camera,
head on. I, half-turned
to them. I am 14.
Now, tears well
as I look.
My father, nearly skin and bone,
his clothes hanging loosely,
his eyes obscured by

the brim of his hat, his belt drawn
tight through the buckle,
the rest hanging loosely,
he, worn by ten years of
menial labour.
My mother in the middle,
flanked by
my father to her right
and me to her left.
They do not touch hands...
a decision has been made. It's
1941 and he will leave
to travel by train and ship
to Argentia Bay,
Newfoundland, venturing on
the Atlantic, a landlocked
farm boy,
to practice at last
his trade, learned
in Connecticut before
the Crash when he
was in his twenties.
It will become his
war effort, age 42.
How ironic his big chance...
to help build an
Allied submarine base
against the increased
presence of Nazi
U-Boats, prowling
the coast and up
the St. Lawrence.
My mother is bereft and angry...
First the Great Depression...
And now, THIS!!!
They do not touch.
And then I see. My mother has

grasped my hand.
Oh, how I remember
my hand clasped
within her own
to comfort the little
child I was, sundered
from the farm, then
confined to
paved sidewalks.
From afar, I sense
the pain of their
wartime sundering and
my early entry
into young adulthood.
For at 14, I became
my mother's comforter,
my young sister's
bedtime story teller.
Phyllis, not yet ten,
missed our father as only
a child at
that age does.
And I? I kept close
to him by becoming
the doorkeeper in his absence,
the last to check
that doors were locked
at night, to keep
an eye on what
was going on
in our crowded
neighbourhood, to carry
the rent money to
the landlord
of our little flat.
A lesson learned early
is for life. I am

still a doorkeeper to this day.
My father taught me well.
One thing I know. Soon after my
father's departure, letter-writing
between them never failed.
Every day a letter arrived,
a letter was sent, for
three years.
They were my parents' lifeline
in trying times.
And gradually, gradually,
a semblance of
peace descended upon us.
Thank you, Dorothy, for you
remember me and
I remember you and together
we remember
the farm homes
we loved so long ago.
Do you see? The negative you sent
became a positive!

Postwar Contrast in Schools

I began my teaching days in 1948 at the Inverness High School in my old Megantic community. All of my people in living memory had attended that school. Although I was a raw recruit to the profession, my introduction to teaching was actually quite smooth and for that I credit my students entirely. Since most of them were related to me, they treated me rather gently. After all, they were not keen to see one of their own turn out to be a flop and disgrace them all!

Behind my coming to teach in Inverness was my grandfather. He was living in his retirement house in the village and his only son, Elmer, had recently died at the age of forty-two. So it was a sad little home. In the meantime, in the spring of 1948 I had completed my B.A. at McGill and was at loose ends. My mother and sister had moved the year before to Toronto to join my father who at last had meaningful employment, working on Toronto's postwar building of high-rises.

My grandfather wrote me a letter suggesting I apply to teach at the Inverness High School, knowing I did not want to move to Toronto since John and I had been engaged while still at McGill. And so began a memorable year living with my beloved grandfather ~ good for him and good for me! While the farm was gone, the community at large was still there. It was a great consolation to me and for John, a chance to get to know the people and the landscape that he had heard so much about.

In 1949 I returned to Montreal after the school year was over and John and I were married in St. Clement's Church in Verdun where, at the age of five, my uneasy adaptation to urban life had begun. After earning the high school teachers' diploma required, I taught for a year at Woodland School where I had begun grade one at six.

In 1950, John had begun theological studies at McGill, after he had worked for two years with Shawinigan Engineering as a Civil Engineer. We were living in McMasterville on the South Shore near two of John's fellow theological students: Bob Osborne, a former teacher and Canadian Army veteran, his wife, Beverley, and their baby, John; and Graham Tucker, another engineer who was engaged to be married to Jean, a nurse. Since such a move required John and me to become commuters by train, I had been granted a transfer to Victoria School on St. Luke Street in downtown Montreal not far from the train station.

In September 1951, I began travelling to Montreal with John, Bob and Graham on the train from the Beloeil station, which was within walking distance of McMasterville. In the city, I parted company with them and climbed on board the Ste. Catherine Street streetcar to Victoria School. In my new school, I happily joined several university friends, including Barbara Jackson, Flor-

ence Murray and Joan Mount, who were already on the staff of Victoria School.

It was still a difficult postwar period ~ children were upset because their parents were upset. Some had lost their fathers, and some were badly affected by parents long separated because of the war and now struggling to form a complete family again. Most of my students lived with their parents, but a small group were in a category of their own. They were the children whose home life had disintegrated, making them wards of the province. They lived in Summerhill House up Guy Street not far from Victoria School. And therein lay the challenge for the teacher: how to relate to such a disparate group.

The problem was not that the classes were too big. On the contrary, the numbers were under twenty-five, which would seem ideal. But Victoria School was in a decline, providing only grades one to six, its very name revealing its age. Next door was a stable belonging to a Montreal dairy where the horses were housed, fed and watered. Every morning they were harnessed and hitched up to wagons in the warm months and sleighs in the winter ~ an image connected to a world rapidly evaporating after World War II.

Once a prestigious part of Montreal, properties on some streets in the area of Victoria School had slid into rental housing during the war. However, the Montreal School Board had a social conscience toward the children. A nurse, Rita Doyon, visited regularly, checking on their health and advising students about good nutrition. "Remember," she would say, "an apple eaten after your lunch will help to clean your teeth."

A dental office was set up in one of the empty classrooms and dental procedures were provided for those in need. As well, from time to time, the board sent a social worker to make contact with disturbed students and a doctor to tend to other health matters. It was obvious that the Board regarded Victoria School as one that needed attention.

At first, for me the contrast between the ambiance of the In-verness School and Victoria School was like the difference between light and darkness. The Summerhill students brought with them an already well-developed class structure of their own in retaliation to the rules of the House, one in particular that they were not allowed to enter a store at any time. In reaction, several girls from Summerhill undertook to enlist girls, not resident there, to shoplift for them. So it was not unusual for classes to be visited by a policeman.

The politics within my class were fierce the first three months or so. Summerhill girls challenged those who lived at home to participate in various schemes and created unrest among the boys -- until the day that the Board arranged to have a sink installed in each classroom! I decided to bring a bar of soap and some hand lotion, and placed them on the back of the sink. I was amazed at the reaction, however. "Oh, Miss, what a nice thing to do!" the Summerhill ringleader said, immediately getting up from her seat to wash her hands and apply the lotion. I was thankful for small mercies.

Shortly thereafter one of the girls brought a kitten she had found mewing by the fence separating the school from the stable. "Please Miss, could we keep it here in the classroom?" Well, it so happened that the principal, Freddy Files, already had a number of pets in the school basement that some of the younger children helped to look after. How could he refuse us having a kitten?

One of the children brought a box from home at lunchtime and soon the kitten was in residence. There was soon a roster of volunteers lined up to look after its needs. Of course, the kitten in its box had to be up front by my desk so it could be observed.

Amazingly, my students were quiet as lambs as I taught. They settled down to work in quiet, and the kitten stopped jumping out at me as I walked back and forth putting an assignment on the board. Soon the little animal was fast asleep.

Then in January 1952, I became pregnant when John was in his second year of theological studies at McGill. Strange as it might seem, within a short period of time four of us young teachers, married around 1949, became pregnant. The others were Florence

Murray, Garnice Ware and Joan Mount Kabayama. The other teachers coddled us during recess and at lunchtime, urging us to put our feet up as the weeks passed.

As for Rita Doyon, she certainly went the extra mile as school nurse, by offering at the home of one of the teachers a 'live' demonstration of how to bathe a baby. How was it live? Marion, wife of our fellow teacher, Percy Lane, had recently given birth to their son, Timothy. He made the demonstration live and didn't seem to mind at all!

When it was obvious I was expecting a baby, my students (both girls and boys) became utterly solicitous toward me. In particular I remember one withdrawn student whose home life had become quite fractious (she had earlier declared that she had changed her name and no longer wanted to be called by her old one.) "Oh, Miss," she cried, "I hope you have a girl and I have a name for her. Name her Dawn, D-A-W-N," spelling it out for me.

On the staff there were a number of teachers with long experience in the life of that school; they became mentors to us younger ones. Lila Cook, from Megantic County, was a contemporary of my aunts. I couldn't have gotten along without her. Another teacher, Una, lived in a lovely family home up the hill and was the soul of hospitality to us all. An after-school tea party in her garden or lunch in her gracious dining room was a memorable event.

As I look back down memory lane to those years, another student comes to mind. She seemed solitary, not making any effort to connect with the others, nor with me. My recollection is that she lived with her family who had recently arrived in Montreal. I don't remember ever meeting her parents. While she appeared turned in on herself, she was nevertheless verbal, often creating a running commentary of her own.

At a certain point, she was withdrawn from the school. Apparently, she already had a reputation as a troublemaker elsewhere. I don't recall her presence in the classroom during the time the kitten was in residence nor when the students became aware of 'the baby that was coming.' Years passed and occasionally she would come to mind; I could not but feel regret.

Very recently, while sorting out the contents of some boxes downstairs, I came across a letter I had long forgotten. The date was 12 February 1952. It was addressed to Mrs. M.L. Buck, 1822 St. Luke St., Victoria School, Montreal, Que. The letter follows:

Dear Mrs. Buck

Just a few lines to let you know I am sorry for not answering your most welcome letter sooner because my arm hurt me very bad.

I like it out here very much. We have all kinds of sports & gym out here. We also have cooking and sewing. In your letter you asked if you can come up & see me. Yes you can come. Every Sunday from 1 - 5 o'clock. I am now in Grade 7 because I really tried hard in school. Oh! Yes about my arm I still have my cast on my hand & it makes me cry every time I look at it. How I wish it were off. Well I guess I am running short of words so I will say Good-Bye for now.

From a girl who likes you & never showed it.

I read this letter I had tucked away over fifty years ago when I was twenty-four. I sat very still realizing that as it turned out, I had not visited her. And then a surge of memory of those often bereft postwar children of Victoria School swept over me. I salute them wherever they are for they were part of the suffering of the innocent, engendered by war.

Fair Exchange: in Memory of Catherine
Teaching adults for
nearly 20 years,
often three generations
in one classroom,
I began at the point where
the end of the '60s

84

touched the '70s
where Decadence and Apocalypse met.
Fourteen years out of the
classroom, John and I having
specialized in sons (four), I longed
to teach again.
Part-time
would be best, the three eldest
all in their teens, the
youngest, only ten.
For decades Adult Ed was
Night School but given
the current times, the age of
Decadence and Apocalypse created
a job for me,
a chance for students.
How come?
A new initiative, Day Classes, to
cast a wider net, gathering
in disaffected teens, some
"drop outs"
for their own reasons, some
younger than 19,
no longer welcome
in regular high school.
(Decadence and Apocalypse, not
nurturing times for the young.)
But the net was
wide, attracting
the middle generation and
seniors, Catherine,
being the first to enroll.
The Board was looking for
accredited, experienced teachers,
free to teach during the day,
twice a week, three hours a day, per course.
This was my chance!

My assignment?
grade 12 "matric", English 30,
my students age nineteen
(some younger) to sixty-seven,
Catherine's age.
A three generational classroom
new for us all.
Of the middle generation, the net,
at first, gathered in
mostly women, their children
all in school ... Moms' chance for
freedom, twice a week, three hours
a day to learn again.
The teens sat beside
no one who looked
their mother's age,
Some middle-age ones, weary,
from the challenge of raising teens
in chaotic times, (something I
could relate to), picked up
again old arguments, better
left at home.
The two generations toyed
with drawing battle lines,
shooting remarks like
darts across the room.
Then the one senior, Catherine,
bamboozled us all:
Standing up, she turned to
look at them. "I've worked
most of my life
at the Calgary
General Hospital, with
young people.
I'm retired now and
I miss them.
At my age, that's all of you.

I'm so glad
to be here."
Silence reigned. Students, abashed.
A breathing space for
us all... Catherine's
peace initiative hovered
over our heads like
a dove ... while Listening and
Learning waited
in the wings....
I stood up.
"Welcome, class, to English 30!"

Lost and Found

I

Crisis and Joy, two sides
of one coin
like the woman
in Luke, the loss
of her silver...
lamp lit, broom in hand
sweep from top to
bottom, corners cleared...
until the moment,
I FOUND IT!!!
Loss of home in childhood
is one too hard to bear
for a child at five
lives in a cloud
o'er hanging all
But does not know
the WHY
THE GREAT DEPRESSION
(What is that?)
Made us land on
hard pavement

live in a tiny flat in a brick block,
three storeys high
strangers upstairs
downstairs
WHO ARE THEY?
I want to go
HOME.
To Grammy and Pappy and all
of us near and
all the rooms
I know so well.
Carlo (he'll miss us) and
Mittens' kittens. And Oh-hh
the barn (the smell of hay)
What will all the creatures
say now we have
gone away?
ONLY VISITS NOW
SUMMER'S OVER
CAN'T STAY ...

II

Time passed ... I reached 15 ...
in high school now
one foot on
the pavement, one
in the fields of HOME... BUT the
heart went out of HOME
as Grammy's heart gave way
leaving Pappy alone
with his ailing son too
frail to work on the farm.
Time passed... I reached 18
farm sold
that summer
an indelible hurt so
deep in the heart

no floods of
tears could erase
and a yearning began
too hard to bear as in
the child I used to be.
The heart too tender a place
to store memories
of what once had been,
but the mind has deep
dark corners that
unbidden will give
them room
Memories inactive, waiting...
as years and years passed.

III

UNTIL my reflective age
breaks through, scattering
darkness in flood of light.
HOW? By means of words spoken ...
Tell us Mother\Grandmother what
was it like that house?
The art of story telling
shimmered at
the edge of light.
The young folk, two generations all
asked the QUESTION, passport
to my MUSE.
The place? In Caragana Cottage,
Calgary, discovered by default,
eight months after our arrival
(when we were not yet forty)
lease on house for minister
suddenly terminated by owner
UP FOR SALE, NO WARNING ...
John and I in CRISIS
four youngsters in school
youngest in kindergarten

WHERE TO LIVE?
A kindly church warden's advice ...
church housing allowance
already there in place
Can you come up with
down payment?
While prices are low
at present (the year, 1966)
prices are bound to rise
NOW a good time to buy
BUT FOR US
NOW didn't seem too good ...
Above all what we needed
was a light to
lighten our path
WHAT DID WE KNOW? That John had
answered a call to
Christ Church, by Elbow Park
The answer to our CRISIS
slowly began to form,
we cashed in our only
stock (CPR),
my parents (not rich) wrote,
"Here is $2000. DON'T PAY
IT BACK! But do the same for
your boys some day."
Leap of faith on their part,
from parents with loving hearts
light at the end of
the tunnel, a pattern to
follow for us.
And we began to look
for a nearby house,
for the boys, no changes
in schools, still near
their friends and close enough
to the church.

IV

I FOUND IT!!!
House for sale
around the corner
Boys at school, John
at work, appointment
made with agent
I rush out the door
to see it...
address in
hand. I stare
at the house...
sloping roof, red
brick chimney, gabled
windows, walls white
blue-green trim
a house of wood,
a farmhouse???
large downstairs windows,
decorated with leaded panes.
Along north side, an
expansive side garden
(like a field!)
enclosed three sides
by hedge of caragana
brought first to the west
by Ukrainians, its yellow blooms
a reminder of home.
the agent arrives
turns the key
in the lock...
I walk in and there
on the very doorstep
I feel a rush of HOME!!!
Then he casually
tells me
It was built in

a field
when Calgary
was young,
the year 1914!!!
SAME AS MY OLD
QUEBEC FARMHOUSE!!!
My heart lifts, yea,
it soars.
I enter the house,
no central hallway
just space to meander
through the rooms
filled with light
through windows north
south east and west
at the centre of
the house, a wood
burning hearth like
the wood burning
stoves of HOME.
Upstairs steep stairs to
rooms with gabled windows
under the slope of the roof.
Caragana Cottage
where our sons grew
to manhood and we
to our old age.
And memories hidden
in mindlessness began
to seek the heart...
MY HOME IN THE WEST
BECAME MY MUSE where
the loss of
my old farmhouse,
was replaced by one
in the west
firmly planted

in spite of
the change around,
a farmhouse in the city
in a portion of that field
abundant still in topsoil
two feet deep, its side garden
proudly blooming for
ninety-one years.
In my heart now an image
the two forever joined.
How bountiful a Muse is mine
that seemed to come
so late in time,
yet, matched with
my reflective age
the stories hidden in
dark of mind, came to light
within my heart.
"Don't ever sell this house,"
says ten-year-old
grandson, John. Look!
there's the little
loose tile on the
hearth. Remember!
I used to carry it round
but I always put it back
You've never cemented it in!
It makes me think of
when I was little, a very
long time ago!
Looking into his face
we give thanks
for our roots in the west.

Crisis and Opportunity

In June, 1966, just over a year after we had arrived from Montreal, a second crisis occurred. Archdeacon Hasted Dowker, rector of Christ Church, retired because of ill health. In 1965 John had accepted an invitation by the Archdeacon to be his associate for two years. When the senior partner, (as in the case of the Archdeacon) for reasons of ill health must retire, the associate indicates, as is the custom, to the Bishop and the church corporation his willingness to discontinue as associate, pending the choosing of and appointment of a new rector.

Several options were open to us. For example, Dr. R.H.L. Slater, John's professor at McGill, suggested he undertake to do PhD studies in theology at Harvard where he, Dr. Slater, was now teaching. In the end we decided to stay in the west. In April 1967, John, as his celebration of Canada's centennial, began to teach in the Maths/Physics Department at the Southern Alberta Institute of Technology for a year, based on his earlier Engineering Degree. There he discovered that the librarian was a minister of the gospel too.

The beginning of a new age was upon us. The phenomenon in the sixties of what came to be known as 'Worker Priests' began in France and spread thereafter to other places, including Canada and the United States. Retaining their licenses to practice their Holy Orders under the jurisdiction of the Bishops and working in the outside world became the dual calling of these priests (ministers). John taught at SAIT for nearly twenty-three years.

At the reception for him upon his retirement, the head of his department paid him a tribute. He recalled that at the time John was interviewed for a teaching position, the committee was not sure what to make of this experienced priest who first had been a civil engineer. During the interview it came to light that not only were John's engineering qualifications an important part of his credentials, his experience with people of all sorts and conditions underscored his empathetic outlook. He was hired.

At the end of his remarks, the head said, "John, as well as your devotion to students, you carried us," as he recalled traumatic occasions over the years when John's pastoral counsel was quietly sought.

At the same time in the practice of his Holy Orders, he traveled many miles in the Diocese of Calgary, taking services in parishes temporarily without a priest and in the case of illness of the priest. Also, for twelve years during the '70s and early '80s, John was active in a Team Ministry of three Anglican churches in Calgary; his designation was Worker Priest. On Ascension Day, May 2004, a celebration of the 50th anniversary of John's ordination to the priesthood was held at Christ Church, Elbow Park, Calgary. Civil Engineer, Anglican Priest and Teacher, one man's tri-fold career!

Parents with Loving Hearts: a letter

Every old letter tells a story and unearthing old letters is an emotional experience. Time rushes backwards with unbelievable speed, taking one out of the present into the past. In the wink of an eye the emotions rise, and for a short while, the span of one's life so far seems to stretch and lengthen in a montage of moments triggered, then remembered.

987 Kingston Rd, apt. 3
Toronto, June 18, 1966

Dear Laurel & John,

Just a note in answer to yours which came this morning. Dad & I have been thinking about what you are going to do and we have a suggestion to make. John, why don't you bring your family to Toronto. Our lease here is up Oct. 1st. We could rent a house with room for all of us and perhaps Laurel could get a job to help out while you are at College and I would be around to

get the boys lunch at noon. We pay $95 a month for apt. & garage and for a little more we could rent a house.

Why not pack up and come along. Our cottage and yours would be very comfortable for the summer and by Sept. we could get the house and the boys could start school. I don't know if this is anything you'd want to do but think it over and let us know or we can talk some more when you get here. Laurel, you might let us know what you think. We think what you are going to do is a good idea and should work out fine.

We had a talk with Phyl and she thinks you wouldn't have to take a course to get into a Toronto school. She says she'd be delighted if you'd come to Toronto.

Well, Folks, I'll say no more for now. How long are you obligated to stay at Christ Church?

Many thanks for the picture. The mountains are grand. I'd like to see them in Summer.

We'll be looking for you at the cottage. Dad is having the last two weeks of July and we'll be there by the 16th. Love to all,

Mom & Dad

Generosity without Bounds

Remembering again my parents' bountiful generosity, I recalled a generous act associated with our McMasterville community. In the same box as my mother's letter, I found one from Kay and Jack Ralph, members of the local Bible Study, which we were invited to join. For the next two years, it became a place of encouragement for the three theological students and their wives.

As the last year of theological studies began, I was eight months pregnant and had not had an income from my teaching since June. From April to September in 1952, John worked as an engineer for the Aluminum Company of Canada on a short-term contract. After returning to his studies, he occasionally was asked to work on checking designs for the company when he had a few hours to spare. But as October approached, our income was sharply reduced while John settled into his last year in which he had to write a final thesis. With seven months in his last year to go, the prospect of our financial situation seemed bleak.

That was the setting of our lives when the following letter from our friends, Kay and Jack, arrived. At the top of the page was printed a line from Acts 2: 28:

Thou shalt make me full of joy with Thy countenance.

Dear John and Laurel,

For the past three months Jack and I have been praying that the Lord would direct us as to what we should do with our tithes and offerings for His work. We both felt that we could not entirely support the church here unless there was to be a definite evangelistic ministry. Three weeks ago as I was sitting in church the Lord seemed to speak to me and lay it on my heart that we could have a very real part in the ministry of the Gospel through one of the boys in training. Some time later I spoke to Jack about it and he said the same thing had been on his heart. So we felt it was surely of the Lord.

Since then we have prayed that He would direct us to the one He would have us give this, His money, to and for some reason He has directed us to John and Laurel.

Will you allow us to have a part in the ministry of the Gospel through you?

In warm Christian Love,
Kay & Jack

For us their wonderfully generous offer was truly a Godsend. We were humbled by such generosity and for their reason behind it. But there was more, all of us Protestants were welcomed into the congregation of McMasterville United Church, because it was the only Protestant church in that town.

That Kay and Jack as Baptists were ready and willing to help 'one of the boys in training' and thereby, 'have a part in the ministry of the Gospel' was certainly an unforgettable ecumenical expression. Some time later when John was launched into his ministry, we found a way to acknowledge our dear friends' contribution to us by sending several donations to the Montreal Diocesan College at McGill to assist a needy student.

Rescuer, Mentor and Friend

In 1947 at the end of my second to last year at McGill, I found a job through the campus Summer Job Placement Service as a waitress at Bigwin Inn, in the Muskoka area of Ontario. To make a little more money, I agreed to go up early to help clean the ceilings, walls and floors, the particular area my group would work on being the Rotunda.

When I arrived I was unnerved at first to find that the walls were high and the ceiling vaulted. Somehow I managed to get out of working on the ceiling and confined my efforts to the walls, standing on a high ladder and not daring to look down.

Bigwin Inn had established its prestigious reputation on Bigwin Island long before the war. In 1947 it had been refurbished after being closed during the war years. The practice of hiring university students from spring to early fall was already established at such hotels as Château Lake Louise and Banff Springs in Alberta. Now Bigwin Inn had resumed that practice.

During that time, students from the west and the east met and worked together. In fact, some of them had already had experience in several prestigious hotels, working their way across the country, so to speak. As for me, my sole experience of such a job was the summer of 1947. Most of the jobs required us to work seven days with the eighth day off. Then we were free for a whole day after a full week of working days as well as taking our turn at night working in the Tuck Shop. To the credit of the Inn's administration, we were allowed to borrow a canoe and life jackets at the dock. And thereby hangs my tale!

Four of us waitresses set off one bright morning in Muskoka's Lake of Bays with its many small islands (Bigwin Island being one of them) to explore the shoreline. Keeping close to shore seemed a wise suggestion, since only a couple of us had any prior experience with handling a canoe. As for me, I was used to a solid flat-bottomed rowboat and two sturdy oars, one on each side. As we passed one island, a couple waved to us.

We had lunches from the Tuck Shop for a picnic on one of the deserted islands. No doubt today most of those islands have cottages on them, but not sixty years ago! We found such an island and pulled the canoe up on shore. The sun was warm. The ground sloped gently toward the shore, enabling us to gaze off toward several nearby inhabited islands as we stretched out on the ground. We were tired but hungry and turned to get out our lunches. Right away we discovered that no one had brought a bottle opener.

One brave soul said, "I know how to take the bottle cap off. See that big rock over there. All we need is to see if it has the right kind of edge along the side to do the trick." It seemed simple. She grasped the bottle of pop firmly, found an appropriate edge on the rock and pressed the cap against it. Suddenly, there was a sound of glass cracking and the girl dropped to the ground, clutching her leg as the bright blood ran down. One of the others grabbed a towel, wrapping it snugly around the wound. None of us had thought of bringing even band-aids.

We were silent for a moment and then we went into action. In a few minutes we had the wounded one in the canoe with a blanket around her shoulders while someone held her steady. All thoughts of a picnic had vanished, as we set out for the island where the couple had waved to us. That is how we met Mildred and Max Russell, the good Samaritans.

As we approached their dock, their teenage daughter had just made a high dive off the diving-board mounted on the boat-house, while her brother was swimming nearby. Mildred must have seen us from the cottage and called Max. In a matter of minutes, our wounded friend was in the cottage with the rest of us following after. Mildred unwrapped the towel from the injured leg but the blood was ready to flow again. At that moment (I regret to have to say it), I fainted, putting the Russells in the position of having to look after two of us.

When Mildred had finished tending to the wound, she suggested that it needed stitches and that the patient should be looked after by the nurse at Bigwin Inn. So the crew (minus me) climbed back into the canoe and, accompanied by Max in his canoe, departed for Bigwin Island, a fairly short distance away.

I soon learned that Max was a teacher at Toronto's Technical Institute and that Mildred was an artist who designed flannelgraphs that could be mounted on a demonstration board for teaching purposes in Sunday Schools. They brought to life, in brilliant colours, dramatic scenes from the Bible that were familiar to many a child in days gone by. I found myself relaxing in the warm hospitality of these people who had looked after our crew member's sudden emergency on the island and then me in my fainting spell.

Later, I came to realize that if I hadn't fainted in the midst of Mildred's tending to the injured girl, the likelihood of getting to know the Russells would, indeed, have been low. During my remaining days of working at Bigwin Inn, I would venture out in a canoe to spend time with them on some of my days off.

Occasionally, John would come to visit me from Camp Borden on his motorbike that summer of 1947. It was at that time that he, too, came to know Mildred and Max.

The reason that John and the other young men were at Camp Borden was a worldwide, ominous one. These men had been around thirteen in 1939 when World War I began. In 1947 they were in their early twenties. Now that World War II had ended, a new threat had risen - the lifting of the Iron Curtain (the spread of Communism), Russian spy networks and fear of the possible use of the atom and hydrogen bombs. The Cold War had begun.

As a result, the Allies settled on the need to get ready a nucleus of young men. All of them studying in technical areas, these men began training as officers in the Canadian Army that particular summer. They spent time at a basic training camp at Barriefield, Ontario, followed by a period at Camp Borden involving the maintenance and use of military technical equipment. An awareness of the possibility of a World War III was not lost upon our generation. Doubtless that is why it seems we grew up fast. Just two years after World War II had ended, a worldwide threat of yet another war certainly focused our minds on what was important.

A search of my box recently revealed another old letter, this time from Mildred Russell, written a year after my Bigwin Inn experience. As letters do, it speaks for itself.

June 13, 1948

Dear John and Laurel,

It was a real pleasure hearing from you and our reply is really by way of congratulations all round. Seldom are friends able to congratulate both parties to an engagement as we are in telling you that we wish you every happiness in this world ~ and the next. We have been enriched in knowing you both, and count you as *friends*. We don't find it hard to remember ourselves at your age, and how we seemed to hold the world in our hands and heaven in our hearts. The feeling grows!

I am afraid we shall just miss seeing Laurel when she returns for July. Your visits at Easter-time carried us over a hard place, and I personally felt that the Lord had brought you both, and Phyllis, to us that day, so full of memories. It is 'Eyes Ahead' for us, and the future is bright with prospect, but sometimes exquisite comforts come to us. I could tell you of many ~ anon.

Max has bought a car, and it is *possible* that we shall call at 63 Corley [my parents' address in Toronto at that time] before we leave. We have a very full program of last minute obligations, such as sick old friends, dozens of flannelgraphs, June's exams (excruciating!), and so forth.

I am enclosing a little booklet in this letter to you, commending some of the fine thoughts contained therein. If you are interested I have many more by the same author more exhaustive. About thirty writings on the deeper things of God. [A publication by the Inter Varsity Christian Fellowship.]

We have enjoyed Phyllis' [my sister] company and hope she comes again before we go away. Well, my dears, time does fly though you may not think it. And my word to you is "Let Patience have her perfect work."

Ever your friend in Christ,
Mildred Russell

As I read this letter, nearly sixty years later, I see what a wonderful perspective on their long, fulfilling marriage Mildred was sharing with us. It was almost like a mother's but at the same time like a friend's. Yet, I see a care not to burden us with their own 'hard place' nor to, possibly, cause us to be anxious about the future in that uncertain postwar period. But to us as a young couple about to embark upon our marriage, Mildred and Max not only gave us hope, but genuinely affirmed us. I salute them both.

Whimsy, Short, Sweet and Sharp

The following letter is a short one, sweet, yet sharp and whimsical, so typical of my old community's humour. It was written by my great-aunt Martha Henderson upon hearing that I was going to teach at the high school for the 1948-1949 term in my old village of Inverness.

Aunt Martha was actually a cousin of my grandmother Jenny. She was petite, stylish in her manner of dress and in old age still had a curly head of hair. She had never married ~ if there had been a disappointment in love in her youth, I never heard of it. She earned her living as a caregiver for many years, as many an unmarried woman did in her generation.

During two or three summers before 1942, when my grandmother died, Aunt Martha, although considerably older than my grandmother, came to the farm to help with her care. She had been a good cook in her day. I recall one summer she began to make a lemon meringue pie. The pie baked and the meringue rose high.

When we began to eat it at supper, there was a stunned silence. The filling tasted sour, though it was laced with sugar, and the meringue, though sweet, had a lingering vinegar taste. We looked at Aunt Martha. "Well," she said, "what was I to do? There was no lemon so I used some white vinegar to give it tartness and sugar to sweeten it up!"

Dear Miss Laurel Canning, [here is the whimsy, poking a little fun at me because of my new status as a teacher]

Congratulations to you on your new occupation at Inverness. May you have every good luck in trimming up any [my students, i.e.] who need the same.

Do not work too hard. I am sending you an apron as you may be at some domestic work. Wish I were there to run in and make Phyl pancakes [my younger sister, very fond of pancakes]. I had hoped to see Bertha to congratulate her [my young aunt, Bertha, who had recently married]. She gave me no chance, as she did not drop a line to say where to find her. Just said she was leaving next day. May have been to North Pole or Palestine. However, I hope to see her some time in the far future.

Be good to yourself. Do not fall in love with the first farmer you meet.

Bye, bye, Love, Martha.

P.S.

This is why Rose [a relative] never wanted Sissie [her daughter and a cousin of mine] to be a school teacher. She said she would marry the first farmer she met. I said, "Oh, not necessarily." Rose swore it was a fact and she mentioned several school teachers around the country who married farmers. [Martha interjected by saying] "The teachers were lucky to get them!"

Should your mother ever chance to see the apron, she will recognize it. I hope she won't take any offence at me giving it away when it is in the family. It is too nice for domestic work I do. I am sending it in good faith. Please take no offence.

As ever, with love,
Martha

P.P.S. I am old fashioned. I believe in aprons as a necessary article.

A Letter from My Father, Looking Forward to Spring...

The last of these letters is from my father, Robert Henry Canning (Harry). It was written on 23 February 1977, a month almost to the day before his death on 25 March 1977. It was addressed to three of our sons: Jack, twenty-two, Stephen, twenty-one, and Tom, seventeen, the first two at university and Tom in high school. Martin and Irene had been married five years by then. Love, humour, wit, and looking forward to spring are all there.

Inverness, Quebec G0S 1K0

February 23/1977

Hello Jack, Steve and Tom,

I want to thank you fellows for the National Geographic which I received. The Jan. issue is nice. I have such thoughtful grandsons. I have been behind with writing for some time as we both had the Flu for nearly 4 wks. Gram is over it now but I've not been out at all for a month now. Sinus and a really bad cough, on the mend now.

We had a nice long newsy letter from Grandma Buck [me] yesterday. So you are finished with college, Jack, in one more year. How does it feel to be so close to the end of your school days? It's a long hard pull, eh? Your Mom said Tom is fine now and enjoying some cross-country skiing. [Tom had sustained an injury when one of the opposing players speared him with a hockey stick in a particularly nasty game.]

We have mountains of snow here in Inverness. We will be glad to see the last of it. Our old Squire Cook passed on last week, poor fellow (at 69 years). Spent over a year and a half in Thetford Hosp., caused by a stroke that completely paralyzed his right side. He had no control of his bodily functions, not funny at all.

Laurel said you had a visit from Martin and Sarah Anne, bet he is a proud Daddy, visiting with his 16 lb. 4-month-old daughter. Your Mom says Sarah is very strong and can stand up if you hold her hand. Wonderful to have such a healthy girl. How does she get along with Macorba? Elkhounds are supposed to be fond of children. Patricia, [my young cousin battling with cancer] has a couple of weeks more of cobalt treatment after her operation. She gets home on wk.ends and is thin but in good spirits. She has plenty of courage. Roger is on his snowplowing job, sometimes twenty-four hours a day. One section of his plowing is in the little village of Pont Briand, the snow capital of Levesque's Quebec.

Sid and Stella [my aunt and uncle] are not so pleased with Inverness. Stella has been sick at Xmas and New Year's. She has had a stroke and sleeps a lot. Sid gets the meals but says he doesn't care so much for cooking and pot wrestling. They have Gram's cousin, Rueben Little staying with them. He has his name in at the Wales Home but has to wait until the Lord takes away some Old Crock before there is room for Rueben. He is a confirmed tobacco chewer and sometimes swallows tobacco juice, a rather awful habit but then he will never have worms! He is 81 yrs old now and still goes for the mail and has several places where he stops in for tea and cookies. Guess where he can drink tea six times a day. A real walking "tea gut".

How is Mart's Fiat coming? [Martin has always enjoyed restoring car engines] We will be going to Red Pine cottage some time in the spring. We don't know which month yet. Perhaps, we can get Sid to move our furniture back to the cottage.

Well I seem to have nothing more to write. Tell Laurel I'll answer her last letter soon. I haven't heard from Irene or Martin if they received the parcel Gram sent. The way Sarah is growing it probably will be too small for her. I'll close for now.

Love and best wishes and like Irene always says, God bless you all,

Gramp.

A Poem: In Praise of Life & Our Home in the West

In old age when the years grow shorter, we long
to know again what once gave us joy.
And then (by chance?) our doctor
just happens to suggest
it's time... to undertake a
new beginning...
Do what you would like, he says
whatever that might be,
it's up to you... (Camping comes to mind!)
the ideal conditions, full moon, soft night breezes, the
tent breathing, the closeness to the earth, the trees
overhead, stirring the air...
the deal is sealed but we hesitate a little
Why does the idea of camping come to us?
So many years have passed since
last we camped with family,
Indeed, we did try camping, just the two of us,
but found it to be lonely.
So we took trips instead, once
camping in Ireland meeting up with Jack, who
had been cycling there, he
in his little pup tent, we in ours, the cows
munching and mooing beyond the fence.
So one warm September day not long ago we
load the van, sleeping bags, foams, pillows and cooler
camp stove, matches, dishes and all.
But the old tent has tears in it from
a bear long ago: we all were camping
in B.C., it was raining...
So in the shelter we were cooking breakfast.
The deed was done by the bear in our absence...
Still, the memory lingers. What if a bear
comes again? What are we thinking of?
Answer...
we'll sleep in the van.
We head south to Nanton, turn west

to Chain Lakes where we canoed so long ago.
Then south on 22, all of it coming back
as clear as day.
And then the sign: YOU ARE ENTERING
THE FINEST RANCHLANDS
IN CANADA. KEEP IT GREEN.
CLOSE THE GATE. Amen to that!
For as many say, Passing through
that glorious landscape is
a mystical, even spiritual experience. Why?
because you come close to seeing forever.
Gently rolling green velvet hills, descending
to valleys full of flowing streams, rising
even higher on all sides
to reveal range upon range of hills to
meet the Rockies. Fields upon fields of
cattle, cows and calves grazing,
ranchers building up their stock
in hopes the U.S. border dispute will settle,
ranch homes and buildings sheltered
by mature trees against winter winds, all
under a living, breathing sky
at play with sun and cloud.
So we reach the crossroads, turn east
to the Porcupine Hills, where gigantic angels
on the summits stand, their wings
wheeling like those Ezekiel saw,
wheels within wheels.
Catching the wind, the 'angels' generate
electric energy, ministering
to our need for light. Perhaps,
not so different from
the ones Ezekiel saw, after all.
So we descend into Pincher Creek, a long
established town,
its gravelly bottomed creek
once panned by men searching for gold.

The name? Northwest Mounted Police
camping nearby long ago, one of them
finds a rusting set of pincers.
The name 'Pincher' stuck,
perhaps, it better reflects
the mood of the gold
seeker, pinched by failure.
So we find a campground beside
the creek, Sleepy Hollow, quiet
except for the murmuring of the water.
The late afternoon sky, high and clear.
Looking at one another, we appear
to have the same thought. Perhaps,
we might buy a new tent,
no bears here, so close to town.
Climbing back into the van, we head to
town, first staking a claim
to our site of choice,
self-registering at the gate.
So a friendly passerby points out
the hardware store. We enter.
"It's late in the season" we hear, "but
we have two or three tents left.
Take a look." And there it is, our tent,
we claim it, pay for it and head back
to make an early supper. It's a high-tech,
dome-shaped tent for two, the supports all
on the outside, blue, grey with a bright orange
logo, named for Orion! And a silvery fly, coated
to repel, not just rain but harmful UV rays.
So at dusk John, pleased as punch with our tent
removes it from the box, gently unrolls it
and sets to work to follow the directions
while I wash up the dishes.
Soon it's put together pitched under
an opening in tall bushes...
Later, (our gear stowed away in the van),

we snuggle into our sleeping bags.
Our bodies relax,
sensing the heartbeat
of Mother Earth
as our First Nations people say.
The night sky vaults over us, deep,
blueblack, signal for the stars to appear.
They take their places gradually...
lighting up the night to tell
'the old, old story'.
Communing with the Creator, we begin
our new beginning...
One last thought comes before sleep,
Communing and Community, from
the same root.
At home the dictionary tells me
Community means Neighbourhood!
Amen to that!

EPILOGUE

Once again, as with *Stream of Memory*, *Roots Beneath the Pavement* and *The Spiral Road*, I have come to the end of my stories. But this time, the feeling grows that I've been accompanied not only by family, present and past, but by others. For there are the strangers John and I have met by chance in our travels (some oousins-come-lately, some turned into friends).

And here I would like to pay tribute to one such very dear friend, Wilma Marshall, who died in September 2005. Northern Ireland is not the same without her.

Other strangers, now friends, were the newcomers to our neighbourhood, like the one who honours what has gone before by requesting some sprigs from our old, established gardens to grow in their freshly dug soil ... and the two little sisters who turn to wave at me before closing their gate.

I give thanks for the gift of story telling my old Irish-Quebec community gave to me, ever old, ever new. In keeping with that thought, I recently told a friend that I've been working on a new manuscript. She replied, "Laurel, you will be writing stories until you go to your grave! And even after that, your stories will come fluttering down from above!" I replied, "Well, I'm glad you said they will come fluttering DOWN."

ACKNOWLEDGEMENTS

To undertake the art of writing takes courage - every writer knows this. For writing is not only a solitary task; it requires taking soundings deep within one's psyche, imagination and memories. My experience as a writer of memoirs tells me there is no way round this process.

Thankfully, there are friendly encouragers, family and friends, who ask, "Are you working on another book?" Then there is my dear life companion, John, who says, "Let me know when you want me to listen to what you've written so far."

But, oh, the day when the publisher replies, "Yes, this means we are going to do it." For me, the effect of such words is akin to that of a pregnant woman in her 9th month. Like her, I find the expectation of fulfillment is palpable. And, so to speak, the publisher becomes the midwife in the birth of a book!

So from the top, my heart-felt thanks to Judy Isherwood of Shoreline, publisher, editor, friend. Sarah Robinson has designed a cover that encourages the readers to 'lift up your hearts'. And I thank Shanti Maharaj and Drew McKevitt for their help as intern-editors.

Sarah Buck, granddaughter and writer, composed the Foreword, making glad her grandmother's heart. Brian Brennan, writer and musician, graciously wrote the piece for the back cover as he has done before.

I extend my sincere thanks to all.

Laurel Canning Buck

Foothills and Sperrin Mountains through cottage windows

MEMBER OF SCABRINI GROUP

Québec, Canada
2006